T-REX
STOLE MY
COMPUTER

plus 29 stories
NOT about dinosaurs

WILLIAM JOHN ROSTRON

Some of these stories happened, some of them didn't
... and some of them *almost* happened.

2022 WRITER'S DIGEST
AWARD
WINNER
WRITING COMPETITION

To my grandchildren

William M. Rostron

Samantha S. Rostron

Bella-Capri Rostron

Ava Marie Brunjes

And my "grand pets"

"Crazy" Alice

"Mad" Max

and

T-Rex (The Bunny)

Because it is always better to have a pet rabbit named
"T-Rex"
… than a pet T-Rex named "Bunny."

CONTENTS

"Can you tell a wise man by the way he speaks or spells?
Is this more important than the stories that he tells?"

"Better Man Than I"
- The Yardbirds

PROLOGUE

T-REX STOLE MY COMPUTER

I am weird! My friends can well document that I have never eaten a single fruit or vegetable in my life. That objection includes all seafood, coffee, tea, and all salads (including potato and macaroni). Additionally, no mustard, mayonnaise, hot sauce, or dressings. Yes, but what does that have to do with the title of this book?

About six years ago, I started to seriously get into writing short stories. By then, I had written three novels and felt I had told those stories to their conclusion. I sought a new writing challenge, and short stories fit the bill. That genre worked out well, as I'd had eight of them published and felt highly confident writing short works. Then came the cookbook.

The anthology publisher required a recipe, directions, and a prequel story about why you picked that item. I chose an omelet. Yes, I do eat eggs. In fact, my one great cooking skill is a perfect ham, cheese, and bacon omelet. It is a tradition that I serve these by popular demand on Christmas mornings. I receive rave reviews for my gourmet work. (It's my story, and I can editorialize...or maybe fantasize.)

I submitted my recipe and story and titled it "Carnivore." It was immediately rejected. I pictured them laughing at my attempt to describe my quirky eating habits. As a defensive response to this reaction, I imagined them as hating omelets...or worse yet, being confirmed vegetarians—maybe even vegans! Of course, they rejected me. They hated me for my ways. It was a clear-cut case of carnivore prejudice.

However, in my heart, I knew I had failed to amuse them. I had lost my mojo. My brief but glorious run as a short story-writing legend had ended. Self-doubt crept into my psyche, and I stopped writing short stories, positive that I could not rekindle the skill.

Assuming I was done, I memorialized published works into a complete book of short stories. If nothing else, all my accepted work would be in one location for my children and grandchildren to read. That book, *A Flamingo Under the Carousel*, received critical acceptance. Yet I knew all those stories had been before "Carnivore." The public didn't know of my fall from grace. My conscience bothered me. Hidden within the twenty-five pieces in that book was a lone story that had never been published—"Carnivore," the rejected poor black sheep of my story family.

I felt I had cheated by including it. However, I had justified my actions by leaving out the actual omelet ingredients and directions and so had purged the evil from its body. Even with this rationalization, I still could not bring myself to write short stories again. So, I wrote another novel, *The Other Side of the Wind*, which worked out quite well. But the writer's block continued as far as short stories were concerned.

Then I got sick. The course of treatment required quite a bit of medication. One of those medications (taken every few weeks) had the side effect of causing 72 hours of insomnia each time it was infused. Yet, it was *not* a bad insomnia but rather a total alertness and energy for that period of time. (Prescribed steroids will do that.)

I tried watching old movies and reading, and that did fill the time. I even emailed my publisher, who answered my messages in real-time (at 3 am). Either she had run-of-the-mill insomnia or was that overworked.

Yet something strangely happened. I started to get ideas—wild and detailed ideas for stories. At first, I scribbled little notes on a pad, but soon, I was flushing them out into 500 to 5000-word stories in the middle of the night. Every one of them was different in theme and texture. Before I knew it, I had the outlines and workings of almost fifteen pieces. But…

The failure of "Carnivore" haunted me. Were these stories actually good, or was I just experiencing drug-induced delirium? There was only one way to find out—submit *the* story again. Yes, I could go no further until "Carnivore" received acceptance. However, I could not do that in its previous form. I needed to rewrite it and give it more. Like the mythological phoenix, from the ashes of "Carnivore," a new version, almost triple in length, was created. A line from that tale became its new title, "Call Me T-Rex." I could do nothing until "T-Rex" proved worthwhile. All computer time became obsessed with T-Rex. There would be no Facebook…or emails…or messages to my friends…or bill paying online…or anything until "T-Rex" was perfected. In reality, that story consumed all my computer time. Yes, "T-Rex Stole My Computer."

The revamped story was not only immediately published but went on to win an award from the 2022 *Writer's Digest* Short Story Contest. It purged my writing demons, thus allowing me to produce the stories you see before you. Once the floodgates opened, many of my stories written in all-night delirium were published …with some also receiving awards from *Writer's Digest* and other entities.

It was exhilarating to get back to that spirit of accomplishment, but more importantly, it is what it did for me. Those inspirations that came to me in my delirium are what got me through six months of a devastating illness. Writing might not have been the cure, but it was undoubtedly a medicine that eased my body and mind.

One final note: No creative genius clued me into the line about T-Rex that got me going. While the fervor of my all-nighters led to many creative moments, it also led to moments of confusion and forgetfulness. My "stroke of genius" using T-Rex was an illusion. I had not come up with it out of the blue. Months later, I remembered that my granddaughter, Ava, had adopted a pet bunny, which she had named…T-Rex.

PART I

❧

IT'S MY LIFE

"It's my life, and I'll do what I want.
It's my life, and I'll think like I want.
Tell me I'm wrong,
Show me some time."

- The Animals

IT'S MY LIFE

꧁꧂

A wise man once told me nobody will read an autobiography unless the author is famous. Taking this sage advice, I never wrote an autobiography because I am not famous—not even remotely so.

Because of this fundamental observation, I have taken most of the interesting experiences of my life and made them into autobiographical fiction. This means that the tales told contain some kernel of reality from which I veer rather radically at some point. However, *this* section of the book is straight non-fiction. What you see is what you get. To put it more bluntly, this all happened.

"Call Me T-Rex" – Background

- *Writer's Digest* **Awards (2022)**
- As mentioned in the prologue, this story has had two lives. First, it was a story included in my first compilation of short stories, *A Flamingo Under the Carousel*. In that publication, it was one of the few stories that had yet to be published before *my* book. I tripled the length and added a

bit more humor. It was not only published but also received recognition from the ***Writer's Digest* Awards of 2022.** The line between success and failure is never more evident when you realize that the first version of this story, "Carnivore," was rejected, and this newer version received accolades.

- Published as "Call Me T-Rex" in the *"Happy Accidents and Other Humorous Tales"* anthology.
- Published as "Carnivore" in *"A Flamingo Under the Carousel"*

"61?"

- Though this tale seems like it should be in the fantasy section of this book, it is real. The events occurred exactly as described during the birth of our son, Jarrod. He's in his forties now, and I still can't explain how events unfolded.
- First published in *Visible Ink XV* anthology (2023)

"Fairway to Heaven" - Background

- I wrote this story half a century ago…but only in my mind. I worked as a caddy for four years to help pay for college. While catering to the rich and famous who frequented an exclusive country club, I often found myself amused. "I've got to write this stuff down," was my constant refrain. But life intervened, and I never did. However, I recently saw a promo for an anthology entitled ***Green.*** Anything that conjured up visions of green could be submitted. My thoughts immediately turned to my years of "looping" (caddy-talk for the job). It all came back to me so quickly. You don't have to be a golfer or even have

any knowledge of golf to get the gist of this humorous (and sometimes serious) romp through the links.
- Publication pending in *Green* anthology in late 2024.

"The Last Chord" - Background

- **Visible Ink Film (2024)** – available for viewing at www.WilliamJohnRostron.com
- This piece was the toughest story of my life to write...and the toughest story of my life to live. Some of the events in this tale may seem familiar to readers of my novels. That is because I used some of the initial actual events of this tale as the basis for writing my four fiction novels. Again, readers will understand how my fictional tale ended. However, I could never predict how my *real* story would end.
- First published in *Visible Ink XV* anthology (2024)
- An alternate version was published in the *Here in the Now* anthology (2024)

"Cat's In the Cradle" – Background

- **Writers Digest Awards (2022)**
- Sometimes, life finds a way to tell you that you did something right.
- First published in *Finding Family* anthology (2022)

"Earl, Mary, and The Yardbirds" – Background

- I am a plagiarist. However, I will never suffer copyright infringement lawsuits because I only copy sections of my own work. Those who have read my novel **Band in the Wind** know that the backdrop of that tale is a group of young men growing up in a rapidly and violently integrating section of Queens, New York, in the 1960s. The protagonist in the book seeks to escape the violence through music. Much of this story is reminiscent of a particular chapter in *Band in the Wind.* However, this nonfiction piece describes the real story of events that changed my life path.
- Alternate version in **Long Island Writers Group Anthology** (Under the title "Catch the Wind" - 2022)
- This version pending publication in **Unsung Heroes** anthology (2024)

CALL ME T-REX

⪽

I had a heart attack… and recovered…and my friends were relieved. Wait. I don't think that I made that clear enough. They were relieved, not that I recovered, but rather that I *actually had* the heart attack in the first place. Don't get me wrong; my friends are not monsters. They also enthusiastically cheered my continued existence on this planet (eventually). However, there was a real undercurrent of satisfaction that I did require a procedure and a short hospital stay. I probably need to explain my friends—and, more importantly, me.

You see, I am a carnivore, the exact opposite of a vegetarian. Most of my friends are not. I like to use the analogy of dinosaurs. In second grade, we learned that some dinosaurs only ate plants, and some only ate meat. Guess which one I am? Just call me "T-Rex." In over seven decades of life, I have never eaten a fruit or vegetable. Instead, I subsist on a diet that relies heavily on long-dead animals. Before becoming my dinner, they may have been a cow, a chicken, or even a pig. I am not extremely picky in this matter, as long as it once had a heartbeat.

Conversely, I have never eaten a salad and consider it a fundamental belief that if God had wanted me to eat anything green, he would have made me that cow, chicken, or pig. The only exception

I make in my prohibition of things growing in the dirt is for starches (some call them carbs)—and believe me, I had to work hard on that one. The potato or wheat stalk must have had a transformative experience. Sorry, no baked potato for me—too close to its original form. It has to have been cut up and then fried to look like a chip, a waffle, or something French (in name, at least). As for wheat—bring in that grindstone, crush it, mulch it, and reform it into any shape you want. Think cereal…pasta…bread.

Just about now, I would expect that any die-hard vegetarians are ready to tar and feather me—and vegans forget about it. Keep your carrot sticks in your holsters. I don't think I had a choice. I often tried to be good and fit in with a healthy society. It just didn't work. I could say that vegetables and my digestive system do not agree. However, that would not exactly be true. They never even get that far into my anatomy. Instead, any green intruders are rejected at the first portal of entry, my mouth. I didn't ask to be this way, but it no longer bothers me. Perhaps my aversion to veggies is due to a mental condition that has its roots deep in some childhood trauma. Or maybe I have some physical anomaly that makes me adverse to vegetables and fruits. Perhaps I will someday see an ad on TV for a drug that will solve my problem. Of course, the disclaimer will include a thousand unwanted side effects, so scratch that. I know mine is not the healthiest lifestyle, but it is the lifestyle I am comfortable with.

I have tried to understand this peculiarity my whole life, and the best explanation for my weirdness is texture. Fruit in its natural form looks and smells good to me. I just can't eat it without some modification. I can drink *fruit* juices, but I cannot consume those same fruits. I choke on a grape but can handle a raisin (especially in Raisin Bran with lots of sugar coating). I can eat some dehydrated fruit if it has been reduced to something resembling a gummy bear. Yeah, I know they also have sugar (which is grown as grass and then pulverized just like wheat!).

Vegetables, on the other hand, are downright repulsive to me. They lack any attraction or redeeming social value. Even now, I am downright perplexed when I watch someone eating a pre-dinner salad. Why are you eating this oversized grass? Why are you filling up valuable stomach space with something I can pick in my garden or walk upon in nature? Why not go straight to the *actual* food?

Eggs are an unusual dilemma for me. You have to admit, they sort of look like vegetables. For me, that could have been game over. However, I will eat eggs scrambled or in an omelet. Of course, a bit of sausage is necessary to assuage my carnivore tendencies. If you think this is inconsistent, you have to understand my reasoning. I have tricked myself into accepting eggs because, in reality, aren't they… well…"pre-chickens." Case closed. Pre-chickens are acceptable.

The first criticism of my eating habits is usually leveled at my parents.

"How did they raise you?"

"How did they let you get away with that?"

"If you were my kid, you would have cleaned your plate."

I responded by saying that my parents were good parents. They did try. However, I often pushed them to their limits. The age-old *"You'll sit there until you eat your vegetables"* resulted in many an all-nighter. I got to know my kitchen in the dark and was often downright obnoxious. (You know us carnivores).

On one occasion, I remember my parents sneaking into the next room to check on me, sitting in the dark. They may have sentenced me to 5 to 10 (hours) at the kitchen table, but they had to keep checking that I was alright. Of course, I picked up on their surveillance and decided to make them feel guilty. As with all carnivores, I have a mean streak. I decided to convince them that my punishment had caused inexcusable brain damage. Then, perhaps, child services would intervene and… No, I really wasn't that mean. I just had a sick sense of humor. Making sure they were listening closely, I started a conversation with the string beans on my plate. To be more accurate, they (the beans) started with me.

"Thank you, young man." (The extremely high-pitched voice of me as a string bean)

"For what?" I answered.

"For…you know…um…not eating me." (The string bean)

"I was starving, but I'm all about live and let live." (I was lying to the string bean! The proof being evident in the leftover ketchup on my plate from the not-so-lucky hamburger). I heard my father giggle and my mother gasp, thinking her son was insane and calculating how the cost of therapy would impact the family budget.

"I think he knows we're here," my father said softly. I figured the game was up, but I had another card to play.

"You know I'm, you know, um, carrying little ones." (The return of the string bean voice)

"Aw, that's cute…twins," I replied.

"Are you kidding? You must think there is something wrong with me. The number's eleven…eleven beautiful little pods." (The string bean)

I may never have eaten a string bean, but I knew what the inside of one looked like and, therefore, took on the role of insulted bean quite well. So, I figured this last bit of conversation would serve the double purpose of saving me the "birds and bees" talk that all my friends were getting.

The light came on brilliantly in the kitchen, and my parents stormed in, demanding to know what was happening.

"Nothing much, just sitting here by my lonesome."

I had them speechless. I never admitted to speaking to string beans. After all, I'm not crazy.

I could go on and on with everything my parents tried, I tried, and even a small army of doctors tried before we all gave up. What good would it do?

How do I survive, you might ask? I drink a great deal of water and, in an insane mid-life crisis, ran six marathons. There was no logic to my thought process other than if I punished myself enough physically, I could withstand anything, even being a carnivore. This fact did prove true as my circulatory system grew very efficient at bringing oxygen-rich blood to every part of my body. However, before you think of following my path, consider the following: my next knee operation will be my sixth, giving me an equal number of marathons and knee repairs.

I follow a regimen of vitamin, fiber, and probiotic supplements that I take religiously. However, before you get your hopes up that I am doing something healthy, I take them all in gummy form, which seems to work well for me.

So, what are the adverse effects of a lifetime of unhealthy eating?

Well, I did have that heart attack at age 65. I must mention here that I was watching a Jets football game during the cardiac event. Any fan of that team will agree that a lifetime of bad eating habits might not have been the primary cause of the coronary at that moment.

However, I lived through it, or obviously, you wouldn't be reading this. The exercise provided by the marathon training regimen had created a circulatory system that allowed my heart to function even with blockages. Tiny capillaries had expanded into more significant pathways for my blood to bypass the cholesterol-blocked routes. I had indeed outsmarted the veggies. Well, not entirely; they got their revenge in the form of the two stents that permanently reside in my heart.

That brings me back to my original point. All the years, I maintained seemingly excellent health while eating unhealthily had upset my friends.

"He's not eating right!"

"That's not fair!"

"You just wait and see what happens when he gets older!"

They loved me but were still incensed that I flaunted their deeply held beliefs about food. I was an insult to nature—an abomination to good sense and logic.

When I *had* the heart attack, their world returned to its axis. There was a God up in heaven, and all was right in the universe. Life now made sense to them.

"See, we told him so."

"If only he had listened to us."

"We are thankful that he lived, but he was asking for it…we all know that."

For my part, I am glad they are happy. I'm satisfied eating as I do. It has to be remembered that there is nothing inherently good or evil about eating meat or plants exclusively. After all, both the carnivore and herbivore dinosaurs went extinct around the same time. So, there is no life lesson to be gained from that.

It is time to accept the inevitable—it's too late for me to change. I am and will always be a carnivore.

~

Story Behind the Story:

- I truly am a carnivore.
- NYC Marathons (1987, 1988, 1989) – Long Island Marathons (1988, 1989, 1990) vs knee surgeries (1990, 1998, 1999, 2004, 2015)

61?

I don't believe in the occult or worry about cracked mirrors or walking under ladders. Additionally, I know that my cousin controlled the Ouija Board and that black cats are just felines with dark hair. I would never waste my money on a fortune teller, though crystal balls make great paperweights. I only knock on wood when it is an oak door and want entry. Friday the 13th is just the day after Thursday the 12th. However, despite all that, something inexplicable happened at one important moment in my life.

My story begins in ancient times, before the discovery of the internet and society's obsession with selfies. It was an era when all electronics were analog instead of digital, and you still had to dial a phone. It was before gender reveal parties replaced hearing a doctor say, "It's a boy." Into this world, our child was born.

My strange story begins six months before that happy day. Somewhere in the middle of the night of her first trimester, my wife was startled awake by a bizarre dream. In that dream, the number "61" kept flashing around the moment of childbirth. When it happened a few more times, we tried to find some subconscious connection. If the due date had been June 1, it would have been 6/1. However, a March birth was expected. Was she setting herself up for 6 pound, 1-ounce baby? When I suggested this, she almost tore my head off (hormones had kicked in). No, she insisted, it was 61, not a six and a one.

On March 20, she went into labor. It was midnight, and I assumed I had plenty of time for the short drive to the hospital. Wrong!

"Now," she screamed two minutes later. Soon, we were in the car, arriving at the hospital at 12:46 am. After parking the car, I ran up the stairs to the waiting room only to find a frantic nurse screaming, "Delivery room…Now!"

As I came through one door, the doctor rushed in from another. The hands on the clock read 12:57 am.

"Baby's almost here. Everyone ready?"

Not me, I thought.

The young nurse responsible for recording the birth acted as a play-by-play announcer.

"12:58 pm…the baby is coming. Yahoo!"

"Don't write that down, nurse. He's not out yet," smirked the doctor.

"12:59."

"Not yet!"

"12…60."

Huh?

Watching my son arrive, I almost didn't hear the *false* play-by-play in the background.

"What did you say?" quipped the doctor.

"What do you mean?" answered the young nurse. The other nurses covered their mouths, not wanting to embarrass their young colleague by laughing in her face.

"What was the time of birth?"

"Oops." She started to cry, but the doctor came over and turned her to see the scene of our happy family enjoying the first minutes of our child's life.

"In the end, that's what matters, not that his preliminary birth certificate does not read that he was born at 1:01 am but at…."

"12…**61** a.m.," finished the nurse with a mortified smile.

∽

Story Behind the Story:

- March 20, 1977 - St. Charles Hospital, Port Jefferson, NY
- Official birth records in the delivery room read "Jarrod William Rostron - time of birth – 12:61 a.m."

FAIRWAY TO HEAVEN

I play golf. However, I never take the game seriously. Part of that is because of my age. If it isn't fun, I don't do it. A missed shot (or whiff) can easily result in an assault of humorous comments. After a lousy shot, I can announce, "You stink" to myself, even before others think it. However, that doesn't prevent the barrage of quips that will follow from my so-called friends.

"Oh, get out the tape measure for that one."

"The USGA is calling. They're revoking your membership."

"If it were me, I would have done that shot differently."

Why do I find humor in the game important? It all began fifty years ago when I was a caddy to the rich and famous. The only difference between them and me now was that *they* did not have even the slightest conception that they "stunk." The other noticeable difference was that they were worth millions, and I was virtually penniless.

I found amusement in their attitudes, and because of my experiences with them, I understood that I did not have to take the game with any degree of gravity.

PART 2 - THEY CALL IT GOLF BECAUSE ALL THE OTHER FOUR-LETTER WORDS WERE TAKEN

I was 20 years old and working my way through college when I carried the bags for Mr. F. I won't use names because I don't know if there is a statute of limitations for a lawsuit for defamation of character. Besides, I just read in the paper that he died a few months ago, and I am told that you should never speak ill of the dead. Suffice it to say that his namesake company was one of the largest high-end retailers of goods from jewelry to patio furniture, and his name boldly stood on every store he owned. However, he was a terrible golfer. He didn't know…or at least admit to this reality. Maybe he even reformed in the years after our encounter. However, on that day, he was an obnoxious sneak.

He arrived minutes earlier than the rest of his golfing buddies—a planned move. He asked (no, make that *ordered)* me into position. Caddies often went 100 to 150 yards down the fairway to accurately determine the tee shot's final resting place. It did not take long to conclude that Mr. F thought the tee shots were a multiple-choice situation. He attempted to hit as many shots as possible before his buddies arrived…and then only claimed the best of these as his own.

The first one went in the water—the second deep into the woods. The third dribbled right in front of him on the tee box, and he quickly picked up the evidence. His fourth shot also went in the woods, but only slightly, so it could be played with little effort. His quest for the perfect tee shot ended when the rest of his foursome showed up and were ready to tee off. As the golfers all came down the fairway, tracing their steps to their much better-placed drives, Mr. F approached me. He made sure he was out of earshot of the others when he spoke the words I will never forget.

"Where are my balls, caddy?"

There were numerous ways to answer that query, though none would be as funny as the question itself.

Do you have any?

Sorry, I can't seem to see them.

I think you lost them.

I was so dumbfounded by the question that I didn't immediately respond. Therefore, he repeated it a bit louder…this time with an obnoxious addition.

"I said, you idiot, where are my balls?" I swallowed my pride because I had college, a car, and a date that night to pay for. However, I never forgot the sheer inhumanity that competitive golf had driven this asshole to.

Expressionless, I pointed to the one playable shot sitting by the tree line. I rejoiced when Mr. F. shanked the second shot and hit a tree…the ball ricocheting into a little pond. (*There is a God*, I remember thinking.) At the time, I was with the other player whose bags I carried. I whispered, "You *really* have no balls now." However, I didn't say it softly enough because Mr. A. heard me. He smiled.

"We all know he cheats…it's why none of us will shop in his stores. Relax, kid, don't take what he said to heart. He takes this game too seriously. This quirk is a significant problem when you play as badly as he does."

His words were encouraging, especially since he dwarfed Mr. F. in intelligence. Mr. F had inherited his wealth and eventually would make so many bad business decisions that the business's *fortune* would fall *off* through the years. On the other hand, Mr. A was a self-made man who had designed the largest expansion bridge in the world at the time. He taught me my first lesson, which is not to take the game too seriously.

PART 3 - FORE YOUR LOVE

My second memorable moment came almost a year later. As my experience grew, I was allowed the responsibility of catering to the more elite members of the club. This honor included caddying for an exceptional hockey player brought to the country club to play in a tournament by his boss—who just happened to be the owner of the New York Rangers Hockey team. Some athletes are good at whatever sport they play. He was one of them. But, again, not wanting to throw shade on someone recently deceased (2021), I will only refer to him by his well-earned nickname, "Mr. Ranger."

Mr. Ranger was a nice guy and played the game of golf exceptionally well. However, his motivations may not have been the same as most other golfers. The tournament being played that day was a "mixed" match. Each team included a male and female member of the club and a male and female guest. The owner (again, no names) was a decent enough player, and to his credit, Mr. Ranger made no disparaging remarks when his boss did not perform as well as he did. On the contrary, he was encouraging and reassuring in every comment he made that day.

It was an act. Mr. Ranger's entire day was a well-planned professional con job. He cared nothing about the tournament. He cared about one thing and one thing only…getting in the pants of his female partner. I have no proof of it, but I believe this woman was brought to the tournament by the member as a golf "ringer." She was specifically chosen for her golf skills.

I must mention that at this country club, the rule of the day was misogynism. Most male members believed women were to be seen and not heard…and did not even want to see them on the golf course at certain times. Club rules did not allow women to have tee times before noon. More significantly, they were stripped of their individuality— their names never being used.

Once "Harry Smith's" wife "Alice Smith" entered the country club bounds, she became "Mrs. *Harry* Smith," losing her own identity and first name. It was as if their only existence was as an appendage to their spouse. This one tournament was a peace offering, offsetting a year of degradation.

Though Mrs. Owner could hold her own with a club, Mr. Owner needed to add strength to his team and, therefore, searched long and hard for a female guest with exceptional golf skills. Of course, when he found her, it did not hurt that she was beautiful. Or was that the plan all along? Her beauty might provide extra incentive for his decidedly amorous player/guest, Mr. Ranger. If that was the case, it worked for most of the day.

Not coincidentally, Mr. Ranger was a playboy. History bears this out—he played the field for over thirty years before marrying at age 50. As a famous Ranger GAG line member, he and two teammates had a reputation for scoring a goal a game. Many of his fellow players wondered if it didn't have a duel meaning. Besides commemorating his hockey prowess, some wondered if Mr. Ranger didn't average a **Girl-A-Game.**

Everything aligned for this to be one of my most interesting days as a caddy. Mr. Ranger was busy all day—playing golf, trying to seduce his partner, and giving dating tips to a certain twenty-year-old caddy. This last part was a bit hard because of his thick French accent. A native of Montreal, French was his first language, and he intended to use this romantic tongue to woo the lady sitting next to him in the golf cart.

My day was spent observing the attempted seduction of this Midwest beauty by Montreal's foremost Don Juan as he effectively laid on the romantic French-accented phrases.

My darl-ling, I will hit zee-ball just for you.

Voila (There you go) or *au-revoir* (goodbye) followed every long shot, and the accent intensified when he spoke to *Miss Beautiful Ringer.* He was polite to me, using *s'il vous plait* (please) when he required a club and *merci* (thank you) when I gave it to him. However, something was off. I had seen interviews with him after hockey games, and his Montreal upbringing was not quite so obvious when he spoke. I came to believe that this was all the actions of a *grand seducteur* (no translation necessary…it is just what it sounds like). Proof of this theory came at the very end of the match.

The team of Mr. and Mrs. Owner, Mr. Ranger, and Miss Beautiful Ringer was ahead by one stroke coming into the last hole. All that was necessary was for Mr. Ranger to par the hole; even one over par would probably result in victory. I knew all this as he approached his final shot to the green. He was far from his team, whose shots had all landed on the opposite side of the fairway. As his caddy and resident expert on the course, I advised him where to put his next shot.

"There is a water hazard right in front of the green. I recommend playing it safe. Hit it short of the water, and then chip up, get your par, and it will guarantee winning the tournament."

"Where is zee glory in that?" He answered me while looking at the woman of his dreams (for that day). He was not going to listen to my advice. Instead, he would impress her with a long shot directly onto the green. He gambled and lost…and it cost the team first place. However, all that paled in comparison to his accidental revelation to me. Upon seeing the splash of the ball in the water, he let go with a stream of obscenities that had no equal in my experience.

"G*d- d#*m, m*%ther-f#*king, c*#ks**king, son of b*t*h, piece of sh*t…" and it was all in perfect English—with no accent. I would say I was stunned, but I had suspected that the thick French accent was merely an act. This fact was confirmed when he looked up at me. He realized the others were so far away that they hadn't heard his faux pas. He quickly turned to me and gave me one of his final directions as his caddy.

"You didn't hear that…get it!" No *s'il vous plait* (please) in this sentence spoken in perfect English. And I didn't mention a word to anyone—until I wrote this story post-mortem. After all, *"us guys"* have got to stick together. Okay, that's not actually the reason I kept quiet. His Ranger salary allowed him to pay quite a big tip for my silence.

PART 4 - LIGHTNING STRIKES AGAIN

Yet even the more serious side of my experiences was enlightening. So much of the time that I try to forget was spent in the "caddy yard," the place where we all waited to be called for our day of work. When and if we were employed on any given day was determined by the caddy master, a dour individual who wielded his power with the demeanor of Hitler, Napoleon, and Machiavelli all rolled into one.

His choice of who would work as a caddy daily was erratic. A person might move down the pecking order based on his clothing choice, haircut, or the way he was sitting in the yard. He seemed to take joy in teasing us as he made his choice, faking a point or gesture before picking his next caddy. I imagined that he had a terrible home life, and these moments of power were huge consolations to his beleaguered self-image. He was the god of the caddy yard.

His choices did consistently follow one pattern. All the black caddies were chosen first. His preferences were not done with any social justice motive but because the black caddies were true professionals. Many of them had been doing the job for decades, and they knew every nuance of golf and this particular course. The rest of us were raw white college and high school boys who were mere novices in our service to the golfers.

However, the caddy master was not interested in moral issues but rather in lining his pocket. Greed was his motivating impulse. I was privy to watching the money being slipped to him as an incentive to secure the best of these caddies. At the time, I didn't understand. After eavesdropping on a conversation, I realized this was only a step above one "master" paying for using another "master's slave." I knew this because I heard their racial epithets when they thought no one was listening.

As for us white caddies, we understood that the best should go first, and indeed, we even hoped to be paired up with one of the black caddies because we could learn so much from them. On the occasion of one such pairing, I learned a profound life lesson.

The round had started quite normally on a sunny summer day. I carried two bags, and Harold took two. Harold appeared to be in his fifties, but he could have been younger and merely looked older because of a tough life. As was typical, we didn't talk much to each other. We had nothing in common.

The day went on, and most conversations were about our caddying responsibilities. We did laugh a bit at some of our employers' golfing quirks. It was just another day trying to make some money to get me through life and college…until it wasn't.

The dark clouds started to cover the sky as we entered the back nine. A smart move would have been to call it quits right then, but it wasn't our call being employees and having no say in matters. Thunder could be heard in the distance on the fifteenth hole, and Harold looked at me. I knew he had something on his mind. Then, right in the middle of the fairway, he laid down the clubs and looked at the two golfers he was servicing.

"I think we should go back to the clubhouse before it gets too bad," offered Harold. Caddies only spoke to golfers if asked, and he was not just speaking to them. Instead, he was making a demand disguised as a request.

"I think we can finish the round," was the response of one of the golfers.

"I'm warning you that if I see lightning, I'm gone," Harold stated firmly.

"Who are you talking to?" answered the apparent top dog of this foursome.

Harold didn't answer and just stared at him. We finished that hole, and as they were about to tee off the next hole, a tremendous bolt of lightning crossed the sky. On cue, Harold dropped the two bags he was carrying and started to head for shelter.

"Where do you think you are going?" screamed Mr. Top Dog.

"I warned you," yelled back Harold. "This is a game...and I am not your slave. I'm a man, and I'm not dying for your game."

"I'll have your job for this," returned Mr. Top Dog.

"You can have it. In fact, why don't you do it right now...walk across this open field in a lightning storm...carrying metal clubs in your hands?"

Harold kept walking. Top dog looked at me and said, "Okay, kid, you pick up the clubs, and lets go."

Now, I was at the peak of my physical condition at twenty years old, but there was no way I could lift and carry four bags fully loaded with clubs. I didn't know how to tell them that.

Another tremendous lightning bolt lit the sky and was followed by a deafening thunderclap. The four golfers immediately ran for shelter, with one of them yelling back to me, "Watch the clubs."

What was I to do? To openly ignore them could mean my job. To obey them could mean my life! Before I could ponder this life-or-death decision, two golf carts drove up beside me. These carts held much older members of the club—people who had been playing in the group behind us and had even heard parts of the screaming match.

"Get in, kid. We'll take you back." I looked at the clubs and was indecisive.

"Leave them there. It serves them right," chuckled a kindly older man I knew was one of the club's founders. "If they say anything to the caddy master, we will embarrass the hell out of them."

When we arrived at the clubhouse, I first saw Harold, who was sitting dry as a bone under the outside canopy. When he noticed me, he gave me a thumbs-up and a big smile. However, his smile was not as big as the one I had to hide as we drove past the drenched foursome Harold and I had left.

Harold never suffered repercussions. Too many people were willing to tip the caddy master for using his services. Thanks to the power and influence of the older club members, I continued even after I graduated college.

PART 5 - WHERE ARE MY BALLS? (MY STORY)

As I sit in my den and look out into my backyard, I am reminded of how my career as a caddy ended…suddenly.

I graduated college in May and was still seeking a full-time teaching job. By now, I was pretty well up there on the white caddy seniority list, and I think the caddy master was even getting some tips for my services.

Teaching jobs were slim that year, so I decided to work as a substitute teacher with the consolation that I would caddy as a backup any day I didn't get called to sub. As summer turned to autumn, this became increasingly lucrative. By the end of September, all white college kids were back in school, and by the end of October, most Black caddies had migrated to the South, where golf was starting its season.

The club was so short of caddies that I worked every day I wasn't teaching. The club had a very unusual rule that required every golfer to have a caddy when they played. This rule resulted in me making double time by servicing four golfers instead of two. No, I had not acquired the superstrength that would enable me to carry four bags. The country club was so desperate that they required at least two golfers to drive a cart. I was also their caddy, and I used my knowledge to help them and handed them clubs from their bag—a sweet job for double pay.

As the autumn grew colder, the caddy choices grew thinner. I knew the caddy master was desperate when he approached me one day.

"If you continue until Christmas, there will be a nice holiday bonus for you."

Wow, great work for now, and a bonus to boot.

Though tempted, I never passed up a teaching assignment, but I worked as a caddy every free weekday and every weekend. With the sub pay, the caddy pay, and the expected bonus, I was making a good living and was hoping to buy a new car. It was a grind, but I couldn't pass up the money. I worked seven days a week until almost Christmas.

There was no bonus. Let me restate that. There was a bonus—it just wasn't given to me. I had been told that the club had changed their minds. But, in truth, the caddy master, in all his greed, had pocketed my bonus. I only found this out when I left that last day. A Pro Shop employee, who was only a bit older than me, waved to me on my way out.

"Hey, how are you going to spend your bonus? My boss just gave me mine. It's sweet."

"No, they didn't give them to the caddies this year."

He looked at me quizzically.

"But I saw an envelope with your name on it. I saw your boss put it in his…."

I knew then that the greedy bastard had kept my bonus for himself. After all, he knew I would either not find out or have no recourse because he was the supreme authority over all things caddy. If I complained, he might not ever let me carry another bag. Of course, he didn't realize that I had no intention of returning anyway.

I retraced my steps, went into his office, and confronted him.

"Where is my bonus?"

"I told you there were no bonuses this year." However, a slight smirk across his face told me everything I needed to know.

"I took it, and there is nothing you can do about it."

And there was nothing that I could do.

I walked out of the clubhouse, never to return. I was frustrated and angry…and seemed unable to make things right. It was cold and dark, and there were no golfers around—there might not be until the warmer days of spring.

On that day, I decided that I would never treat anyone like he did me, and even more so, I would never allow myself to be treated like I had been. I would never be greedy, and I would never allow greedy people to fool me. I vowed never to forget that day and decided I needed something to engrain those feelings in my mind.

It is now fifty years later. I play golf once a week—weather and health permitting. Sometimes, I go out in my backyard and take a few practice shots. I use wiffle balls, so they don't travel off my property. I always hit from my makeshift tee box. Like all tee boxes, it is adorned with three large marble globes. The colors are universal—blue for the top players, white for men, and red for women. It is an unusual sight in a private backyard. They are most commonly found on professional golf courses…like the one I stole them from fifty years ago.

My theft was perpetrated to remind me not to be a victim of all the greedy, deceitful people in this world. More importantly, it continues to remind me to treat all people like I wish to be treated.

～

Story Behind the Story:

- Fresh Meadows Country Club – Great Neck, NY – 1967 to 1971
- To this day, the three tee markers sit in the backyard of my Long Island home.
- Comments about my bad shots ("Love the One You Whiff") can be attributed to my golfing buddies Norm and Mac.

THE LAST CHORD

I met Gio the summer I was ten. At first, our friendship centered around stickball, egg creams, and watching cheesy 1950s sci-fi movies. Then, in colder weather, our stickball bats were used to play air guitar, accompanying our favorite records. It was Gio who had the idea of playing actual instruments. We purchased two guitars, $20 each, from a Sears catalog. At first, by virtue of being silent, the two stickball bats might have sounded better.

After many attempts, we figured out how to play the Searchers' "Love Potion #9." Into the night, we played that one song repeatedly while Gio pretended we were in front of an audience.

"Yes, we can play Love Potion #9."

"Oh, you want to hear it again."

"And again!"

Imagination can only take you so far when your entire repertoire is one song. Our night ended when my father threatened to make our guitars into "$40 worth of kindling" if we didn't stop.

We did stop that night, but our musical careers did not. Electric guitars, a drummer…and enormous amounts of practice made us popular enough to tour the metropolitan area. The night before playing at a club to audition for a record contract, Gio and I realized we had a problem. We were underage. Yet, with so much at stake, we didn't hesitate to go ahead. Our plight inspired us to write the first lines of a song. It was a song we never completed.

When police swarmed the venue, we realized we had gambled and lost. Our dream died that night. This caused Gio to leave New York in search of a new life. I was gutted to lose my best friend.

It was decades before we found each other and renewed our friendship by phone. We talked, laughed, and rehashed the good old days from a distance.

Finally, in 2023, we reunited at my Long Island home. While our wives became acquainted, we naturally picked up guitars. Gio's hands formed the first chord of that song we had long ago hoped would be the key to our futures. Suddenly, his hand fell to his side, and as much as he tried, he could not figure out what to do.

"Vascular dementia," whispered his wife as she entered the room. "He doesn't remember much…but he remembers you."

I cried. I cried for our lost years, for our lost friendship. I knew we would never play our song for the record executives or even our wives. Gio had played the last chord of his lifetime.

A month later, Gio had deteriorated to the point where he didn't recognize anyone. As his wife took a break, I stood by his bed. He stared at me blankly. I held his hand.

I thought of how we had never gotten our chance to complete or perform our song fifty years ago. I whispered to ears that I only hoped could hear and understand, "I finished the song for us…for you." I softly sang to him.

Thief

We were living lives of passion,
Never wanting to go slow.
Never thinking about tomorrow,
Never choosing to say no.

We had the promise of a dream
To keep our fates at bay
Then, then came the Thief
And took it all away

In time, time takes everything,
As memories fade to never
How long will he steal from me
This Thief of my forever.

～

Story Behind the Story:

- Though much of the song is based on a 1999 poem by my daughter, Brittany Rostron, some of the original music was written in 1967—the night before the Driftwood Club raid. The opening stanza of the lyrics was written upon the occasion of my learning of "Gio's" condition.
- "Gio" is a fictional name used for the sake of his privacy.

CAT'S IN THE CRADLE

When my mom passed away a few years ago at almost 96 years of age, my sisters and I had the task of emptying a life's worth of belongings from her apartment. The chore of sorting through almost a century of memories was gut-wrenching enough, and emotions were raw. It was then that a particular song started to play on the radio.

A child arrived the other day,
He came into the world the usual way.

So many memories flooded into my brain about family--my relationship with my parents as well as my relationship with my children. The song criticizes a parent who is too busy to be with his child. The son in this tale constantly asks his father to do things with him, only to have the father reject him because he is doing other things. However, the son always holds out hope and responds,

I'm gonna be like him,
You know I'm gonna be like him.

That could have been my parents. It wasn't. Even as my mother grew to need more and more of our time in her nineties, we gave it to her—not out of any sense of obligation, but rather because we wanted to. We had learned that from both my mother and father.

Ironically, as the song still played in the background, I found the yellowed copies of every article I had published in the last forty years. She had placed them in a box after showing them to her friends. I am glad that I made her proud because she was the one who always insisted that I get a college education, even if it meant that she and my father had to work multiple jobs to help me do so. It meant a great deal to her that I fulfilled my dreams because she could not fulfill hers. My mom had wanted to be a teacher, but the Depression deprived her of that. However, she became our teacher, always having time when needed. When my sisters and I were grown and had families, she always had time for us. And still, that was not enough.

Until the age of 86, she continued working in the Suffolk County Community College library. She helped students do their research in pursuit of the degrees that I know she valued so highly. When our entire family tried to dissuade her from working, her answer was simple, "I don't need to do this. I do this because I enjoy being there with the kids and helping." She had hit upon the definition of a teacher. Even though she had been there for us whenever needed, she eventually fulfilled her lifelong dream. I would not be singing "Cat's in the Cradle" for her.

My father never earned a degree and did not even graduate high school. Instead, he chose to join the Navy at age 17, eventually rising to Chief Petty Officer. He had a golden opportunity for advancement because he had been in the Navy before, during, and after the conflict. However, it would have meant months at sea away from his family and a deleterious effect on his children.

"When you coming home, Dad?" (The Son)
"I don't know when, but we'll have a good time then." (The Father)

Instead, my dad took a job that could have been more exciting, well-paying, or prestigious. But it allowed him to be my baseball coach, take me swimming, and enjoy all those nights we watched T.V. together and laughed.

And even more importantly, he taught me the power of reading. Despite his lack of formal education, he always had a book in his possession. When I was young and enamored with the newly popular phenomenon known as T.V., he always insisted that it should not replace the habit of reading. Even with no formal education, he taught me, a smug, know-it-all pre-teen, about the power of the written word. With a pleasant voice and calm attitude, he got through to me with his time and patience. I grew up reading incessantly and spending three decades teaching reading and writing.

"Can you teach me to throw," (The Son)
"Not today, I got a lot to do" (The Father)
"That's okay." (The Son)

No "Cat's in the Cradle" for my dad either. He somehow had time for that catch even after working two backbreaking jobs. And when he got home too late for a nice sunny day at the beach, the whole family instead sat in the dark around a campfire at the shore, laughing and telling stories well into the night. Somehow, my two parents had known how to do it right. We never had money, but we always had each other and a good time until the very end of their lives.

As the song ended, I had a slight smile on my face. Indeed, my mother had died surrounded by four generations of our family, and every one of them *wanted* to be there instead of being *obligated* to be there. However, I felt sad for the father in the song. In the end, his lifetime of not having time for his son resulted in his son not having time for him when he became an adult. He, indeed, had become like his father.

"I'm gonna be like you, Dad,
You know I'm gonna be like you."

So why was this song such an emotional minefield for me now? Why was it so engraved in the fabric of my being? I jokingly always tell anyone who will listen that my Baby Boomer generation should have been called the "Sandwich Generation." With our parents living well into ages thought impossible before modern medicine made it so, my generation had the pleasure and the responsibility of seeing them through their advanced ages. When my parents were younger, Social Security was created, and the age set for collecting was 62. There was a reason for this—that was the average lifespan in the 1930s. By the turn of the 21st century, that lifespan had become almost 80. I laugh at the number because the last members of my family to pass away were aged 95, 96, 99, and 106. They were the top of my Baby Boomer sandwich. The bottom slice of that sandwich is our children.

Most of the members of the generation who reached adulthood in the 1950s and 1960s would leave home by their early 20s. However, for economic and social reasons, most of the generation raised in the 1970s, 1980s, and 1990s stayed in the nest longer, married later, and started careers later. That may be a good thing. However, that did create the bottom of the sandwich, which found the Baby Boomers as the lunch meat in the middle. I don't compare myself to Bologna often, but it fits. And it doesn't bother me. However, in my case, I wanted that sandwich to be perfect. I wanted the bottom to be just as good as the top. I wanted to be as good a parent as I had had. That brings me back full circle to the "Cat's in the Cradle" song.

Harry Chapin wrote the song in 1974, and it became the number-one hit on the charts in December of that year—exactly three months before my first child was born. I don't think that I am alone in the fact that my wife and I obsessed about what kind of parents we would be? Would we make all the right moves? Would we be firm yet tender enough with our children? Would we give them the tools to succeed or at least help them find happiness?

And would we make mistakes? Okay, over time, you realize that all parents make mistakes. The key is learning from them and trying to make them manageable. Yet, listening to that one song on the eve of the birth of our first child stirred the hearts and minds of us very young parents. I knew every verse, and throughout our three children's youth, I would murmur the words to "Cat's in the Cradle" to myself when I needed to decide about priorities. Do I go to his game or go out with my friends? "Cat's in the Cradle." Should I rest from a hard day or listen to a 4th grader play saxophone? "Cat's in the Cradle." Do I do long-needed repairs on the house or go to the beach with the family? "Cat's in the Cradle."

These were relatively easy choices. To be honest, I enjoyed the ride. I wouldn't give up the decades of sports, concerts, camping, and so much more. And yes, even reading them stories about little boy blue and silver spoons.

> *The cat's in the cradle,*
> *And the silver spoon,*
> *little boy blue and the man in the moon.*

I won't tell you it was easy. We offered our children a full life, and they took it: sports, music lessons, and extended family vacations. I realized what this commitment meant on a specific day in 1988. My wife and I looked at our religiously organized calendar of obligations. In that one month, our three children (13, 11, and 7) were scheduled to play for eleven different teams and take three sets of musical lessons weekly. My wife and I had to decide if it was too much—were we spreading ourselves and them too thin? Ultimately, we realized that if we decided which activities to cut, we might choose incorrectly. However, each child would eventually pick their path and follow it, and the array of events would somehow be whittled down to only the most important.

I remember driving with one of my sons to a game over an hour away. After a rough soccer match, the drive home found him sound asleep in the passenger seat. It was then that *the* song came on, and I started to sing along. He woke up from his nap and asked, "What's a cat's cradle?" Thinking I would pass on one life's lessons, I relayed the song's meaning. He looked at me like I was crazy and went back to sleep. However, he must have heard at least some of what I said because he relayed the story to his mother, brother, and sister at dinner that night.

> *A child arrived just the other day,*
> *He came to the world in the usual way.*

My children are grown now, in their thirties and forties, and have children of their own. We recently all got together to enjoy a holiday. Eventually, the first cousins started to play by themselves, and adults relaxed around the table. I noticed a calendar hanging on the wall, just teaming with scheduled events: swim meets, piano lessons, Taekwondo classes, and so much more. Meanwhile, the conversation turned to the upcoming week with my other two children, who were discussing the upcoming volleyball game against a traditional rival, the guitar lessons, acting lessons, and so much more that they all had to attend.

My wife and I sat back and smiled quietly, reliving our own experiences of being stretched too thin.

Finally, after holding in my amusement for a while, I half-jokingly remarked, "I don't know how you all do it?"

However, I don't think they knew I was being sarcastic, and all three of my children turned to me at once. They smiled at each other. Their expression betrayed that a conversation on this matter had occurred at some time in the past—perhaps many times.

The first words out of one of my son's mouth were almost a cue for the other two. He held up his drink, and my other son and daughter clinked glasses with him as all three said, "Cat's in the Cradle, Mom and Dad, Cat's in the Cradle."

∼

Story Behind the Story:

- Harry Chapin's "Cat's in the Cradle" was number #1 on the charts in December of 1974.
- Justin Daniel Rostron was born – April 30, 1975.
- The first "Cat's in the Cradle" discussion was in October 1988 on the way home from a travel soccer game in Auburndale (Queens), NY, with son Jarrod.
- May 2021 – "The Toast"

EARL, MARY AND THE YARDBIRDS

In 1964, just as the Beatles were triumphantly conquering the hearts of American teens, Cambria Heights, the neighborhood I was born and raised in, was poised for the dissolution of its way of life. Located between the overwhelming black neighborhoods of Hollis, St. Albans, and Jamaica and the solid brick wall of the costly areas of Nassau County, the residents developed a siege mentality. Pressed from all sides, they found themselves with very few options. It would take one loose brick, and their fortress would crumble.

Officially, it was just a road called Springfield Boulevard. However, no one on either side of the two-lane blacktop road did not know that it was "the line." With a few rare exceptions, everyone west of the line was black, and everyone east of the line was white. Of course, there were genuine racists on both sides of the line. However, what made this time different was how many people felt nothing but fear: fear of violence, fear of change, fear of property value decline, fear of the unknown. Therefore, blacks and whites kept to themselves, without ever venturing to the other side of the line except at their own risk. That was until the change.

In those days of pre-civil rights consciousness, racism was rampant. Politically incorrect terms such as "negro" or "colored" would have been preferable to what white Americans called African Americans behind their backs...or even to their faces. To white boys in white neighborhoods in the segregated boroughs of New York City, this was not an issue that came to their minds. When they used the phrase "eeny- meeny- miney- mo," it was *not* a tiger they imagined catching by the toe! Yet even the racial slurs that lingered in their daily speech did not always reflect any deep-felt belief system to most pre-teen and teen boys who spouted them. They very often simply mimicked what they had heard their elders say. They knew nothing about and cared less about the affairs of the world. That all changed when the world came knocking on their door.

The schoolyard surrounding P.S. 147 was the center of white teenage social life in the Heights. Whether it was stickball, handball, softball, or goofballs, it was going on there. The very young, with their innocent athletic pursuits, mingled unnoticed with gang-related and vastly horny mid-teens and the burnt-out, strung-out late teens. It was all happening at the yard.

In its infinite wisdom, the City of New York had finally decided to spend some of its tax dollars to redo the schoolyard of P.S. 147. New blacktop, new softball fields, and the construction of basketball courts were an effort to improve the lives of the area's young people. Unfortunately, the politician who came up with this pork-barrel legislation had either never been to the site or was highly misguided in his integration attempts. Blue-collar white kids of primarily Italian and Irish heritage did not play basketball in Cambria Heights. They had no practical use for these new courts. In fact, they resented the loss of space from the handball and stickball courts sacrificed for these unwanted hoops. Yet, their reasoning paled compared to what they viewed as the other undesirable result of the changes.

The beautiful, newly constructed courts served only as a beacon of temptation for "the line" to be obliterated by the influx of young boys of color from the other side. It would not be long before the invisible barrier of Springfield Boulevard was breached, and the conflict began.

Indoctrinated by the pressure tactics of the realtors who stood to make incalculable profits, many white adults reacted to the influx of "them" by putting their houses up for sale. However, the young, hormone-engorged white males viewed this challenge to their turf as a call to arms. Unaware that their parents were in the process of pulling up stakes and heading for the white suburbs of Long Island, they prepared to fight to the death against the encroachment of "outsiders."

And this is where I enter the story. I was fourteen in 1963 and lived just one block east of "the line," thus giving me a front-row seat to most of the violence. Like most young males in Cambria, I knew how to fight and, therefore, was heavily recruited by the local gangs for service on the front line. I would say I went AWOL, except I never enlisted. I never became a part of the violence by choice. I didn't believe in the cause because of three factors: Earl, Mary, and the Yardbirds.

Following a path many in my area took, I spent my high school years in a Catholic high school. I also spent those same years commuting by bus and train to get there. A young man got on the same bus as me every day—only *west of the line*. His name was Earl, and we not only went to the same school but were in homeroom together for four years. He was one of the nicest guys I have ever met. How could I justify the violence and hatred proposed by many of my friends based on race? If this one person could be so good, this dispelled any racist argument of inherent evil. Earl was an example of what every boy or man, white or black, should strive to be…perhaps even more than he needed to be.

In Catholic high schools in the sixties, we all had to wear jackets and ties to school every day. However, it didn't take me long to realize that Earl's shirts were starched, and his jacket and pants were always newly pressed. As a friend, I asked him about it, and he gave me a quizzical look that insinuated *that I really should know the answer.*

"How many black guys are in our grade?"

"Two," I answered, embarrassed that this number was two out of 325.

He looked at me with a small smile and said, "You see what's happening in Cambria. You see what's going on in the world. My parents believe that everything about *us* needs to be perfect…just to be equal. I won't give anyone an excuse to look down on me."

"I don't think that way about you."

"Yeah, but you're just a little shithead." He laughed boisterously. As part of his "perfect" facade, he had never used even innocently stupid language. I guess this was his way of showing that he could let down his "perfect" guard to me because we were friends. I was honored.

As with many of my friends in those days, I lost touch with Earl after graduation. A few years ago, I looked at our alumni directory. Earl was a doctor at a preeminent medical facility.

Then there was Mary. To be specific, Mary Weiss.

Many a young man throughout America lusted for Mary Weiss, the lead singer of The Shangri-Las. Her long blonde hair and pouty grimace that appeared on album covers only increased the sales of these "girl group" phenoms. In an era of The Shirelles, The Supremes, and what seemed like a thousand other groups singing about their devotions to the opposite sex, the Shangri-Las remained the musical version of the "Great White Hope." Not lost in this image was the fact that these girls sang about a life they knew about first-hand from growing up in Cambria Heights.

In the press releases accompanying the group on tour, the group was mentioned as coming from "a rough section of Queens, New York." Unlike most images fabricated for the record-buying public, this statement was true. The people of Cambria Heights knew how rough their area was, and they had watched and listened to these hometown stars sing about a life that they shared in common with the group.

Before stardom, the girls had hung out at Ed's Luncheonette on Linden Boulevard, and the words to many of their songs were autobiographical. However, the real "Leader of the Pack" did not die as in the song "Jimmy" was one of their boyfriends. Yet, even as the Shangri-Las were singing about gang life in Southeast Queens, the scenery rapidly changed to something they would not even recognize when they returned from touring. Their life had been a story of white-on-white violence that was reminiscent of a fifties scenario that was rapidly fading away.

The stories they sang about were fights between the guys who frequented Ed's and their rivals, Renos'. Their battles had been legendary in the eyes of all the young white boys growing up there. But the Renos' and Ed's gangs no longer existed. They had gone extinct in a changing world. Their members had gone on to jobs, families, and life. They had grown up. This maturity had left a void in the gang arena. There was no one left to "defend the border."

New types of gangs in Cambria rose from the ashes of these two groups. Gone was the "hanging out" in a dinette replete with milkshakes and girls. Gone was any social aspect of the memberships. These new gangs would have their origins in the schoolyards and basements throughout the neighborhood. It would include those who attended the local public school and any of the dozens of Catholic high schools in the area. It would not be exclusive but rather inclusive of any guy who wanted to defend himself from what was viewed as the imminent destruction of their home and neighborhood by integration.

Yet, not everyone thought of the Shangri-Las in terms of the gang lifestyle. A small group of Cambria teens emulated another side of their story. I was one of those who saw a group of kids who had made it out of the neighborhood…and they had done it through music. Mary and the rest of the Shangri-Las became the people I wanted to model the direction of my life after. I tried to escape the violence with music.

I rebuffed all offers of gang membership, choosing privately and publicly to use the excuse that I had no time because of "the band." My band progressed, which is a story to be told some other time. However, Mary had shown me the way. To this day, song lyrics always crowd my brain and influence my thoughts. And it all started with emulating Mary Weiss and the Shangri-Las.

Music, and one song specifically, affected me beyond all boundaries of logic. It spoke to the issues of the time and helped me clarify where I stood. It explained to me why Earl's demeanor had made me different than many of my friends who had turned to the ugly side of racism. It changed my mind…it changed my life.

"Better Man Than I" by The Yardbirds had a particular refrain that repeatedly stated… sarcastically…that you were a "better man than I" if you could believe certain concepts. Like "Can you tell a wise man by the way he speaks or spells? Is this more important than the stories that he tells?" and "Can you tell a bad man by the pattern on his tie?" And then the line that put it all in perspective to my fifteen-year-old mind.

Can you condemn a man,
If your faith he doesn't hold?
Say the color of his skin,
Is the color of his soul?

Then, Mister, you're a better man than I.

No! Racism and hate were not acceptable under any circumstances. The anonymously sarcastic "better men" of the song were wrong. They weren't better men than me. I learned that from Earl, Mary, and The Yardbirds.

~

Story Behind the Story:

- The trip from Cambria Heights to Archbishop Molloy High School, Briarwood, Queens, NY, required a bus and train ride. I got on the Q3A bus at its initial stop in Cambria Heights. Earl got the bus at the Cambria Height/St. Albans border.
- Earl and I were in home rooms 1H, 2H, 3H and 4H. We played on our intramural basketball team that won a championship in freshman year. Earl was a star. Putting it nicely, basketball was not my best sport.
- Mary Weiss passed away in 2024. She was a class act to the end. She was working on a show featuring the Shangri-Las' songs.
- The Yardbirds were an English group that incredibly had included (at different times) perhaps three of the greatest rock guitarists of all time: Eric Clapton, Jeff Beck, and

Jimmy Page. (Beck and Page briefly played in the band together.)

- The lead singer of the group, Keith Relf, died of electrocution while playing an ungrounded electric guitar. He was 33 years old.
- "Better Man Than I" was written by Mike and Bryan Hugg.

PART II

DEAR MR. FANTASY

"You are the one who can make us all laugh
But doing that, you break out in tears
Please don't be sad if it was a straight mind, you had
We wouldn't have known you all these years."

-Traffic

DEAR MR. FANTASY

Perhaps it was just too many hours of watching *The Twilight Zone* with my father on Friday nights that colored my vision. Even when writing fictional stories resembling actual events, I tend to create some bizarre slant to the tale. In this book section, I allow that inner crazy man to be unleashed.

Some of these stories contain a kernel of my life, while others put my spin on something I have seen, heard, read, or even written. Many of these nuggets were outlined during the delirious periods I wrote about in the prologue.

"Sea of Heartbreak" – Background

- Can Computers take us to places and times we never dreamed possible? This tale is written in a genre I like to label as autobiographical fantasy. (I think I just made that up.) Even though this is a tale of an imagined scenario, it has its roots in actual events. Have I confused you?
- First published in *Tales of the Sea* anthology (2022)

"Lost in a Lost World" – Background

- Survival seemed impossible on such an alien planet, and indeed it was. I have always wanted to write a story about space exploration.
- First Published in **Shoot for the Moon** anthology (2022)

"Mystery of the Yall" – Background

- A very unusual tribe is discovered in the unchartered section of the Amazon Jungle…and they speak English!
- Publication Pending in **Blue** anthology (2025)

"Pete's Place" – Background

- A story of one man's journey to…
- Ah ha, therein lies the mystery. I briefly thought of making this part of a novella. Though this story stands alone, it is intrinsically tied to two short stories found in *A Flamingo Under the Carousel* ("Crossroads" and "Ghost in the Guitar.") If you have that book, you might reread those stories. However, it is not necessary to enjoy this tale.
- First published in **Darkness Falls** anthology (2022)

SEA OF HEARTBREAK

⚜

Seasick? I understand the concept because of that one disastrous cruise we took. My understanding was further intensified by my inability to make it from Long Island to Connecticut on the ferry without any physical reaction. Seasick—I understand it. What I don't understand is feeling it while sitting in my den staring at my computer!

Is there a connection between seasickness and computers? After all, I am busy reconstructing my family tree on Ancestry.com and oddly finding generations of sailors. Before the woozy stomach developed, I almost started singing Jimmy Buffet's "Son of a Son of a Sailor." Ironically, the words seem ridiculous. "The seas in my veins, my tradition remains." So what's that all about?

It's not that I don't love the sea, especially since I live on Long *Island*. Water surrounds me, and there are hundreds of miles of beaches. That's just how I like my saltwater...around me—while I sit on my butt in the sand looking out at it. I want to see the sea—not be *on* it.

Thinking back to the origin of seasickness, I realized it started when I located my father's World War II records. He was in the navy for six years, stationed on an LST heading for the possible invasion of the Japanese mainland. Those LST ships had front ends that opened up and allowed the attacking soldiers and armaments to charge the beach directly. LST stood for something about that function. However, my father told me the sailors believed it stood for a long, slow target. With the massive total of troops on board, many of these ships were the focus of the Japanese Navy and Air Force. Far too many of the LSTs were sunk by these forces.

That's how far I got in my research when the seasickness prevailed. While staring at the records, I started to see white. Then, I had some stomach pain, and the world got blurry.

While I understand that you may want to have me committed once you hear my story, I will relate what happened next anyway. First, I started to hallucinate (a new seasick symptom indeed). Then, I found myself actually *on* the LST! Japanese planes were diving into the ship and creating havoc on its deck. Meanwhile, I could discern at least one submarine at a distance waiting to unload a torpedo. Casualties were being taken on board, so I ignored my seasickness, embarrassed that my minor foible even existed in light of these injured sailors.

I wondered how the ship would hold out against this barrage. More selfishly, how would it affect me? Though no one noticed me, I felt like I was there. It was not like a dream or even a hallucination anymore.

Then, in the air, I heard a new sound…a different sound. Before looking up, I knew this was the hum of American planes coming to the rescue. They fought the Japanese Zeroes to a standstill, and the enemy eventually disengaged. The submarine likewise fled in the face of attack.

As I looked around, I saw the carnage the attack had wrought. However, nothing could impede the ship's mission or even slow down its speed. The only price paid had been in human lives, and the surviving sailors reverently attended to those bodies.

The wounded all streamed in the same direction, which I assumed contained the sickbay. I followed. There, I found organized chaos. The doctors were overwhelmed with severe injuries while their assistants triaged the wounded, deciding to send them on to surgery or bandage them. While looking at these assistants, I drew back in shock. I should have known. I should have understood then why I was in this illusion, this hallucination, this dream…whatever the hell it was. I saw a pair of hands nimbly and expertly stitching and bandaging a shrapnel wound. The *same hands* that would place a bandage on *my* cuts and bruises a decade later. As I stared at the name tag on his uniform, I realized I would be born and given this same name five years later, with a "Junior" appendage at the end. I could swear he looked up from his mission and smiled at me. But that couldn't be…

I was back at my computer, the seasickness subsiding rapidly. Dare I go on? I never knew or met my paternal grandfather and had no knowledge of his life. However, he was next on my research list. I trembled as I considered the possibilities into which I could be drawn. Imagine if this relative was something less desirable, like a gangster or a serial killer. Would I enter into that world with my "seasickness?"

The only mention I had ever heard of my grandfather was that he abandoned the family in 1930. My father was eight at the time. My grandparents and father moved to New York so my grandfather could seek employment in the merchant marine. That was the last time anyone mentioned his name. "Fred" had essentially disappeared from the human race as far as I or anyone related to me knew. Now, it was my job to solve the mystery.

I don't know which came first, "the seasickness" or the astonishment of what I found. At first, it was a simple internet find… Fred had worked on a ship heading from New York to Amsterdam. So, he was trying to earn a living in the depression. But why had Fred never come back to his family? As the documents revealed the course of his life, it became evident that he may not have done right by his family, yet Grandfather Fred was indeed a brave and heroic man. Between 1930 and 1955, he made 37 Atlantic crossings. These included trips from 1939 to 1945…while German wolfpack submarines tried to sink every ship bringing American goods into Europe to aid the war effort. These unarmed ships were sitting targets for the Nazi predators in many cases. However, the merchant marine job was as necessary as any in the armed forces. I realized that unbeknownst to each other, my father and grandfather were on the seas doing important work at the same time…on two different oceans.

I should have expected the "seasickness" to afflict me then, but I was still surprised when it did.

The slow, lumbering vessel I found myself on seemed almost deserted. I peered through a porthole to see most of the crew engaged in dinner. I was immediately thankful that there were no diving-bombing planes or menacing submarines. I walked the deck, keeping close to the railing in case I needed to upchuck my last meal.

Eventually, I saw two sailors on watch while the others ate their meal. One appeared extraordinarily young and, if I judged correctly, somewhat frightened. The other looked to be in his late forties—just the age my grandfather would have been in 1944. It had to be him, or why would my "seasickness" have brought me here? I approached them. Like my experience on the LST, I did not seem to be visible to them.

"Fred, I'm damn afraid. I got a wife and kid home and wouldn't have signed on if I didn't need the money for them. I keep thinking that there's going to be a torpedo on the horizon and that we're all going to die in this forsaken North Atlantic graveyard."

"You can't be thinking that way," declared the older man, Fred, who I assumed was my long-lost grandfather."

"Why the hell not?"

"I've made this trip thirteen times each way...and I'm still here."

"For how long? I was just listening to a couple of officers talking. Us merchant marine guys have a higher death rate than the guys in the United States Army or the Navy. It's just a matter of time. Maybe I should have joined the army instead."

I was drawn closer. No one had ever mentioned that being in the merchant marine was more dangerous than in the army. I am a history buff and had never heard that tidbit of reality. Now Fred stared down at the young man and thought carefully before speaking.

"You don't want to be doing that," whispered Fred, his thoughts intensely swirling in his head.

"Why not? What do you know about the army? You have been on this ship for the entire war?"

"This one."

"What does that mean?"

"Dammit, don't you young folk study history in school anymore?

Exactly thirty years ago, the same countries were in a war…France, Germany, England, and eventually the U.S."

"You didn't…."

"Yes, I did. I signed up as soon as I was old enough. And I wasn't even an American citizen. My family had come to the United States in 1911 from England. I came of age just as our country joined the war."

"But you look fine. You survived."

"Yeah, but I was only there a few months before it ended. It was enough time to see what hell really was. The mustard gas, the trenches, the land mines…the sheer carnage."

"But you did come home to your family alive."

"*I* did."

The way he emphasized the "I," I knew there was much more to my grandfather Fred's story. I moved in closer because I could feel that this was what I was doing here. I needed to know what he was going to tell the young man.

"The war started in 1914, but not for America. My family had just come from England three years before, so my older brothers felt a duty to join the fight when the country of our birth immediately entered the war. My older brother John sailed for England and joined their army in an elite group known as the Hussars. Unfortunately, he was wounded in his leg. When he recovered, he was sent back to the front lines, where he was again shot in the leg. This time, he lost that limb."

"I can see…."

"No, you can't! My brother Harry turned 18 in 1916. He couldn't get to England because of the submarines, and America was still not in the war. So, Harry joined the Canadian army. They knew how to evade the submarines well enough for him to get their troops across the Atlantic safely."

"Did Harry make it?"

"Yes and no. At the battle of Vimy Ridge, his unit ran head-on into a gas attack. Harry's lungs were so damaged that he still could not breathe right, even after being hospitalized for two years. Like my brother John, he was an invalid for the rest of his life. They are both gone now."

I cried as I heard the story of my two great uncles, but I knew this story was ending. Fred spoke one last time.

"Look out there as far as you can see… what's there?"

"Water."

"Right. It may not be everyone's choice, but I will always choose the sea."

"What do you mean?"

"We're in a God-forsaken war. We could be victims…just like John and Harry. But I don't want to live being carried around by my friends and relatives or not breathing well enough even to take a walk with my children. Out here, if we are attacked, either we live or die…there is no in-between. That's the way I want it."

I understood, or thought I understood, why my grandfather never returned to his wife or child. As irrational as it may seem to me or most people, he never wanted to leave the sea.

It would be all or nothing.

I was back at my computer with the remnants of watery eyes from Grandfather Fred's story still drying. I had had enough genealogy/seasickness for a lifetime. I looked forward to hanging out with the living people who made up my close-knit group. Would I tell them of my experience? Probably not. Not if I want to keep living in my home and not some institution, complete with a straight jacket.

As I am about to shut down all the programs on my Mac, I see the familiar leaf on the Ancestry program. That means they had found a connection that, before now, had been hidden. Should I click on it? Just one more time?

The cold water pierces my skin. Hypothermia is rapidly setting in. Another hallucination? An illusion? A dream? No, the water is too, too cold for that. I cannot even feel the seasickness because I am so numb that I feel nothing. Can I die in this make-believe world? I try to find a reason for my imminent demise but can't. My English ancestors came over by ship in 1911 without incident. My Italian ancestors made the trip ten years before that date without significant problems.

I look around for clues as if knowing the why of my situation will help out. Hundreds of drowned or frozen bodies float in the water around me. I now feel sick to my stomach, but not with the self-absorbent seasickness of before, but rather with revulsion for what I am witnessing around me.

I see a ship in the distance…sinking. Did I jump from its deck? If so, it could not have been long ago, or I would be dead or make-believe dead. Who knows? My last vivid thought is that it is no wonder I hate ships and the ocean.

Consciousness is leaving me as I see what looks like a lifeboat heading my way. Wait! Can they see me? An arm reaches out to pull me into the half-empty boat. As my sides scrape the oar holders, I start to bleed. I don't care. I am in the lifeboat and safe. Why is this experience different from the others? Perhaps because I didn't find my ancestor? Maybe he or she will find me?

I hear loud explosions, and everyone in my rescue craft gasps… screams…and cries. The ship…their ship…my ship(?) is going down. The others have wrapped a blanket around me, and I am content to sit quietly. Yet, my curiosity is overwhelming. If I watch the ship go down, will my dream end? But I have seen no relative! There is no genealogical reason for my near death.

"They said this couldn't happen," shrieks an inconsolable woman. I hear other people in other boats screaming in a cacophony of distress and terror. Yet I am most moved by the woman next to me who murmurs, "God rest their souls."

I cannot resist any longer. I look…just in time to see the stern rushing to join the rest of the ship in its watery grave. The victims remaining on board are now jumping into the vortex created by the rapidly sinking ship. My eyes fix on one singular tragic figure as he plunges past the word "Titanic."

This whole situation is crazy. No one in my family was on the Titanic. No one even knew anyone on that doomed vessel. How do I know this? I am still here. Safe but freezing on this lifeboat in the frigid North Atlantic. Why?

It seems like days, but it is really only hours that we float on the lonely frozen sea before seeing lights in the distance. I know some of the history of the tragic events in which I am now involved. The sinking Titanic contacted many ships, and most did not respond for fear of the very iceberg that had punctured the side of the "unsinkable" ship. Only one vessel responded to rescue those set adrift. It must be the HMS Carpathia in the distance.

I remember reading Walter Lord's book *A Night to Remember* at age ten and being struck by something interesting in the true story of the sinking of the Titanic. However, all the details of that book were washed away by the Hollywood blockbuster movie of the same name. This epic movie rewrote the history of the Titanic, and all I can see and remember are Leonardo DiCaprio and Kate Winslet…and the bodies floating in the water. They got that part right.

The Carpathia closes in on us. The rowboats flock to her light like moths to a flame, a flame of promised warmth and safety. Our turn comes soon, and I climb the ropes to the waiting deck. Real hands touch me and assist me to a spot on the deck, where I am given more blankets, food, and water. The crew works tirelessly under the direction of one man who supervises every detail of the rescue. As he personally ministers to many disheveled, starving survivors, his voice is never silent, commanding others to do likewise. And then he passes me by. He stops…looks back at me for a split second…and smiles. He is then on his way.

Who is he? I stop a crew member passing by, point at the leader, and ask that question. He laughs.

"You'd never know it, but that is our captain…Capt. Arthur Henry Rostron."

Now I remember why I found the book *A Night to Remember* so interesting six decades ago. The captain of the Carpathia and I shared the same uncommon last name. I knew why I was here.

Immediately, I found myself sitting at the computer—all the physical ailments I had had only moments before were gone. I walked over to a bookshelf where I kept all the volumes I had read in my life that I had found fascinating for one reason or another. I took *A Night to Remember* off the shelf and quickly leafed through the pages to the book's center, where there were photographs. One caption read, "Captain Arthur Henry Rostron of the Carpathia. Responsible for the rescue of all of the survivors of the Titanic." I saw the resemblance.

∼

Story Behind the Story:

- Though this is a work of fiction, author William John Rostron is related to Chief Petty Officer William John

Rostron, Sr. (LST)...Fred Rostron (merchant marine and American Expeditionary Force, WWI...John Rostron, Her Majesty's Hussars, WWI...Harry Rostron, Canadian Army, WWI...and Sir Arthur Henry Rostron, Captain of the Carpathia.

LOST IN A LOST WORLD

$\mathcal{S}$

*I*t all went so very wrong. The planning for our space voyage was superb…at least, that is what *they* told us. Nothing could go wrong…*they* told us that, too. However, *they* will never know how screwed up everything became because all lines of communication were destroyed when we crashed on this god-forsaken planet. *They* will never know that their minute calculations had been for naught. *They* will never know that we all died.

It all started so exceptionally well and with such enthusiasm, even though we knew it would take us three years to get to this nearest inhabited planet. There were six of us, interestingly all male. They never explained that anomaly, but the rumor was that they feared an onboard romance (like that couldn't happen with men?) or, worse yet, a pregnancy. As I said, *they* never told us.

Perhaps more interesting was our designations; instead of using our names (which could be long in some cases), we had numerical code names to simplify all messages. Indeed, the cardinal numbers were coded for ordinal numbers representing importance to the mission. I was insulted. The pilot and co-pilot were "1" and "2." The ship's doctor, who doubled as a psychology expert and morale specialist, was "3." The Biologist/Anthropologist was "4," and the sociologist/cultural expert was "5." I was number "6," the linguist. Okay, I understand the pilot being "1," but without me, what good were all the others?

I spent over ten years studying the languages I heard over radio signals sent through space. I had reviewed them diligently to make myself fluent in the most common languages of this alien planet. I should have been called "Number 2." However, in the end, it didn't matter because "1" through "5" are gone, and there is no intelligent life on this hellhole for me to communicate with. Did our scientists miscalculate which planet the messages came from? Or, on the other hand, did the meteor that hit us on approach knock us so far off course that we did not even land on the world that was our destination? I'll never know. Number 1 and Number 2 died instantly on impact. My colleagues Number 3 and Number 5 lingered a bit longer but soon succumbed to fatal injuries...that left Number 4 and me.

I soon realized that, ironically, we two were the best suited to survive this disaster. Number 4 could understand the physical components of this world better than any of us, and I could speak to any beings we came upon. But, of course, that was my ego talking. Where we intended to go, there would have been intelligent life. Where we ended up—not so much. We had detected life forms numbering in the millions, maybe in the billions, where we were supposed to go—most of which were housed in carefully constructed buildings. Yet, looking around me now, I see nothing. No words in my language or the language of our destination planet could describe what we viewed before us. How far off course were we? We wracked our brains for clues to our whereabouts. We tried to reconstruct our final moments in space.

"Readying our approach to the final destination," announced the pilot.

"Roger that," answered the co-pilot.

"How long?" I think it was Number 5 who yelled in anticipation.

"Approach could be a day-long affair," answered the co-pilot. "We must search for the large cities we believe are here."

"Not to mention that those signals could have been coming from the adjoining planets in this solar system. So, Number 6, you better start monitoring the radio to get a more precise landing location."

That order by the pilot is what saved my life. My communication booth was thickly padded with insulation to aid the acoustic properties of my location. No sooner was I settled in my cubicle than Number 4 popped into the seat next to me.

"You have to see what is…." It was the last words spoken before we crashed. The pilot had spotted an object approaching the ship at a rapid rate. He assumed it was a meteor, but I will always wonder if it was a missile sent from below to destroy us. However, the fact that there does not appear to be any intelligent life down here will forever leave my theory unproven.

Now, Number 4 and I found ourselves without food, water, or tools. We had escaped the ship with the clothes on our backs. We had pulled Number 3 and Number 5 from the wreckage, but their wounds were catastrophic. Perhaps if we had been able to hydrate them or mend their injuries, they could have survived. However, we had nothing, and the person who would have known what to do, Number 3, was one of the patients.

We looked everywhere for water but only found unusual formations. Liquid with a beautiful blue color surrounded by a reddish hue on the edges seemed to have the composition of water, but when Number 4 bent down to drink from it, he found the contrary. He did considerable damage to his hand as he cupped it and dipped it into the liquid. Luckily, the burning sensation hit him before he could place the liquid in his mouth. However, his scalded hand immediately began to blister, and we had no way to cool it down. His pain grew as we searched endlessly for a water source to both soothe his wound and quench our thirst. Yet I could not help but notice the beauty of this pool of danger.

We trekked on, looking for something to eat or drink. If this proved impossible, we would surely die. We next came upon a fantastic sight. It was a natural formation but reminded us of an ornately carved staircase. An entire hill seemed to flow with colorful, heated mud sliding down its steps. Water, minerals, and limestone were being heated below the ground, boiling over the top of the hill and flowing down its natural rock steps.

Being a scientist, Number 4 guessed that the main components of this beautiful mixture were water and calcium carbonate, a substance we frequently used at home as an antacid. It might be cool enough to drink if we could find a pool separated from the flowing, heated main body. So we searched the edges of the vast mud waterfall until we found a small pool in the shade. Insane with pain and thirst, Number 4 threw caution to the wind and drank from it. His smile told me it was safe; however, as I lowered my head to drink, he let me know its taste was horrendous.

Our joy was short-lived. Number 4 now removed the cloth with which he had bandaged his hand. The burnt area had become infected, and it seemed like it had now spread up his arm. I was a linguist and knew nothing about this kind of problem. However, the look on his face told me that he was in trouble. But, perhaps, if we had medicine...

"It's too late," he whispered. "I can feel that it has spread farther than you see."

"Let's keep going. Maybe we'll find somebody...or something."

We didn't. Number 4 died the next day. I was all alone.

~

Starvation was driving me to madness. Then, too late for Number 4, I found a beautiful, fresh, flowing water stream. I wouldn't die of thirst. I wish I knew how long I could go without food. I roamed for a couple more days, becoming increasingly weak. I passed more pools of colorful hot water, sometimes gushing out of the ground. Finally, I concluded that this entire planet must be a crust of dirt built over a burning cauldron of a hot core. How else could I explain what I was seeing?

Yet, if there were freshwater, logic told me there must be life forms...and I was proved right. At first, a rumble in the distance drew me in. Over the hill was something, and it had to be good because right now, anything that changed my situation had to be an improvement.

I was almost crawling because I was so weakened by hunger. And then I saw them. Where had they been hiding for the last six days? How had I not run into one of these creatures before—and now I saw thousands.

Anything that walked on four legs at home could be considered a food source. These creatures had four legs. However, they dwarfed me in size. They appeared to weigh about ten times my weight and had huge and dangerous horns on what appeared to be their heads. It was suicide to hunt one of these, but it was also suicide not to. As I grew weaker and weaker, I would not even have the option to pursue the herd.

I found a large stick and looked for one of these animals that had strayed from its group. Perhaps they were docile and killing one would not be difficult. Maybe I could make a fire with some primitive form of friction. But unfortunately, I was getting ahead of myself. At that point, I resolved to eat raw meat to get my strength back. But were these animals even edible meat?

I approached a smallish one that seemed set apart from the crowd. By small, the young animal probably only weighed four times my weight. I clubbed it over the head. I drew blood, but he only stared at me in confusion. It was then that not only did he anger, but larger members of the herd also did. I saw the foolishness of my ways and started to run. Now, there were no thoughts of food but rather survival if I could reach the tree line.

At first, I was far ahead of them, but they rapidly made up the distance once they got going. As the lead animal closed in on me, I made a sharp veer to the right, and he ran right past me, stumbling a bit as he did. However, the second one was upon me before I had time to gloat at my maneuver. I could feel my starvation sapping my strength as I attempted the same move on the second beast. Too slow. One of his horns punctured my right side as he lifted me off the ground and hurled me a dozen feet. Satisfied that they had enacted revenge for my brutality toward their youngster, they lost interest and returned to their herd. I should have been happy that they were not carnivores. However, I was bleeding profusely, and my left arm was at a crooked angle. I soon realized my desperate action in attacking one of the beasts was a fatal mistake. I knew that I did not have long. I struggled to reach the tree line, hoping, at least, to be comfortable in the shade in my final minutes or hours.

I have recorded my saga using the communications equipment

provided. But who will ever hear it? Who will ever come to this horrid planet? Why would they?

I know that I do not have long. My senses are failing me. I swear I can hear people speaking. So I'll use my last ounce of energy to crawl further—to a clearing in the woods.

Is that a signpost? I am a linguist. I have learned the languages of the planet that we were supposed to explore. However, there was no way from radio communication to know what their written language would look like. This sign has twenty-three symbols spaced into three unequal groups. Does that mean it is three words? I crawl a few more steps to touch the sign. The letters are indented, perhaps carved into the wood. My fingers follow the form of the first symbol—two straight lines converging at a point and then proceeding downward as one line. What does it mean?

I hear voices…or do I? I am fading fast. My blood loss is robbing me of any rational thought. Am I imagining hearing the voices spoken in one of the languages I studied so hard to learn? I will leave my recording unit on. Maybe I will be able to listen to it later if I feel better. Yes, maybe later…maybe…

"Welcome to your tour of Yellowstone National Park. We will be making multiple stops to see the many wonders of nature. 'Old Faithful' and the other geysers are just part of the fantastic displays to be viewed. Yellowstone lies on an ancient volcano that creates the fumaroles and mud pots, those beautiful but dangerous multicolor hot springs. And that's not to mention the Mammoth Mud Falls made of calcium carbonate.

Finally, we hope to encounter just some of the thousands of bison roaming the park. However, do not get too close—they can attack, and their horns can fatally wound you. Please be extremely careful out there. Remember that Yellowstone is very different from most places on Earth. It is almost like being on an alien planet."

~

Story Behind the Story:

- All the flora, fauna, and landscapes exist as described in Yellowstone National Park.

- However, beauty is in the eye of the beholder…and point of view is everything.

THE MYSTERY OF THE YALL

I didn't meet him until he was dead. I hope that didn't sound ghoulish. It was just that I wanted it understood that my only knowledge of what he experienced was through the small journal that survived his long journey out of the Amazon. How I wished I could have talked to him about the Yall. Were they real or a product of a fever-racked delusional mind?

As a cultural anthropologist, I was intrigued enough to investigate his claim. If he wrote it down, there must be some basis in fact. But was I correct in this assumption? Could the uncharted, secluded backwaters of the world's largest rainforest hold a genetically Caucasian tribe that spoke English?

I was investigating the effects of the recent drought on the indigenous people of the basin when I became aware of Donald Colson's death. Though I knew of him, we had never actually met. Moreover, I wasn't exactly a fan of his research, which included the disappearance of Percy Fawcett in 1925.

Fawcett was a British army officer turned explorer. He had been investigating the jungles of South America when he went missing. He had been seeking a lost city called "Z," an advanced society deep in the jungles near Matto Grosso. His story was made into a book and then a Hollywood movie in 2016. This kind of notoriety demeans the research of serious anthropologists. However, Donald Colson still went in search of "Z." Unlike Fawcett, Colson did make it back to civilization…barely. Now, all that is left is his notebook, and therein lies the intrigue.

Almost a century later, Donald Colson claimed to have found the bones of Percy Fawcett. Though I disagreed with his attention-seeking quest, I knew that my colleague did have consummate skills when analyzing the physical attributes of Percy Fawcett's skeleton. Unfortunately, however, his analysis showed that the explorer had perished soon after he went missing. So, where did this leave me in my understanding of the lost white tribe?

During the original Lost City of Z expedition, little was made of Percy's eldest son Jack accompanying him…and Jack's bones had never been recovered. However, local natives told legends of a fair-skinned baby girl born a few years later. Following information provided by the Kalapalos, the last tribe to have seen Jack Fawcett alive, Colson's party investigated a burial ground close to the Upper Xingu, a tributary of the Amazon. There, they found a gravesite containing a baby and a native woman. Modern technology proved that the baby shared DNA with the younger Fawcett. Colson also was made aware of an unsubstantiated claim that the baby had a twin who survived.

Colson set out on his third quest with many questions. Was there a second baby? If so, what happened to her? And even if there was a second baby, how could that genetically half-Caucasian baby produce an entire tribe that appeared to be white? The bloodlines would have become diluted in a century. Still, Donald Colson claimed to have discovered a whole tribe who were Caucasian…and spoke English. But he had never found an answer before his death, so now Colson's quest had become mine. I set off with a team.

We followed the Amazon, trying to match landmarks with the descriptions given in Colson's journal. We looked for unusually formed trees, rock outcroppings, and blue water. This last one was the key. The Amazon's water is brown, with occasional areas labeled whitewater and blackwater. What the Amazon River does not have is blue water. Except…

The Yall lived along a tributary of the Amazon—that was blue!

According to the journal, the intersection of this blueish water could be found hidden under a waterfall.

We searched for weeks, investigating every form of water that might loosely be defined as a waterfall. We had wandered far from the Matto Grasso area, and still, we searched. Yet what were we searching for? A possible half-Caucasian infant and her father who somehow transversed miles of jungle and found refuge somewhere? And if the baby had survived to adulthood, how did she do so?

We were nearing the end of our third week of searching when we spotted it—the blue water! Most water's color merely reflects the sediment in or under it. This blue-tinged water retained its color even as we held it. We looked for its source and could not easily discern it. Numerous tributaries were at this location, so we needed to explore each to find its origin. On our third try, we noticed the water becoming bluer as we progressed until we saw it—a stream flowing under a waterfall. We quickly put tarps over all our possessions in the boat and powered ourselves through the waterfall. If we had not known that there was an exit, we would never have entered this watery cavern. However, soon, we were rewarded by intense sunshine and bright blue water on the other side. The cyan-tinged water and the dazzling emerald vegetation gave us the impression of an otherworldly experience. Our wonderment was interrupted by a contingent of natives on the shore.

We were immediately startled by their appearance. Though their hairstyles were as different as those in a cosmopolitan area, it was obvious that the actual hair color was light, primarily brown or, in some cases, blonde. Their skin, though darkened by the rays of the sun, remained lighter than most natives of this entire continent. Their height bordered on tall for both males and females, and their facial features were sharp and angular. I had just taken all this in when...

"Hello, strangers, welcome to the land of the Yall. We are the children of Redbird."

∼

I was dumbstruck and had so many questions. Where could I start? Does anyone remember Donald Colson? Were these people related to

Percy or Jack Fawcett? Where the hell did they get the blonde hair? But instead, I blurted out a stupid command that sounded like something from a cheap science fiction movie.

"Take me to your leader…your chief."

"No, chief, we democrazy," one blonde proudly stated. "We vote for a leader, just like in Amar-Rica."

I understood him even if his pronunciation was slightly off. I realized that this version of the language was shaped by a century of isolation. I should have taken the time to plan my investigation, but I couldn't wait.

"Where did you people come from?" He looked at me like I was insane.

"Here," he answered. The small crowd that surrounded us all laughed.

"Why are you called the Yall?"

"When Redbird came here, he called all people the Yall."

"Where did 'Redbird' come from?"

"Our ancestors tell us that Redbird came down from the sky. Before that, he was with the Brown Witch in Usaland."

Though he mispronounced it (again, that century of isolation), it was evident that Usaland was the United States…and Amar-Rica was America. These clues told me specific facts and confused me even more about others. These people had nothing to do with Percy or Jack Fawcett—all of their references aligned with America, not the United Kingdom.

"Enough questions. Redbird taught us that good ghosts offer food to their friends, and you are our friends." I assumed he meant 'hosts,' and we soon found ourselves getting ready for a feast. They told us that we were being served South Freed Chicken. But, of course, I didn't see any "free chickens" or any other kind of chickens. They were some local birds, and I guess they were free, but as the old cliché goes, it tasted like chicken. They were served with a heavy helping of cassava, which had been mashed to almost resemble mashed potatoes and covered with a "gravy" that consisted of the drippings from the "chicken" and some other nameless ingredients.

Over dinner, I pursued my questioning, though they were more interested in being good (g)hosts than being investigated. However, I persisted.

"Who was Redbird?"

"Redbird was the first man."

"Then who is the first woman?" He smiled but didn't answer my question, instead offering me more food.

"Try more of South Freed Chicken."

"Who is the mother of all men?"

"Oh, that easy question…Nina, wife of Fredbird, son of Redbird."

Now, I needed clarification. Apparently, there was no memory of Redbird's mate. So, did they believe that Fredbird was spontaneously conceived and born? The family tree of these people went through Fredbird and Nina, and Redbird became an almost mythical deity who had appeared one day and was imbued with more of the attributes of a god than a human.

Our conversation intensely involved the South Freed Chicken and the blue water feast that day. The blue water was served in two forms…natural or with a horrible-tasting additive called *mommo*. We hated it and took our water pure. However, the Yall seemed to acquire an almost addictive taste for the *mommo*.

And so our stay with the Yall went. They were kind and friendly people who just happened to be shrouded in mystery. They were a giant puzzle, and I couldn't put all the pieces together.

And then the dying began.

About ten days into our stay, our party of eight started to experience acute symptoms. Headaches and dizziness soon evolved into stomach pain, nausea, and vomiting. Some of our group had abnormally fast heart rates, while others had fevers and aching muscles. We all felt fatigued. Perhaps the one symptom that we all shared was extreme thirst. We, therefore, drank vast amounts of blue water.

I searched Colson's journal for clues and found that all of the members of his expedition had suffered a similar fate; therefore, I assumed that something in the area was causing our problems. My conclusion led me to the *mommo*. Though we preferred our water straight, occasionally, we would join the natives in their favorite drink. They had developed an immunity to the effects of mommo. I immediately ordered our expedition to stop consumption of the *mommo*-tainted water. Perhaps the pure water would wash whatever was ailing us out of our system.

It didn't work. On the fourteenth day of our stay, the first four of our group died. The Yall did everything possible to make us comfortable, but they seemed unable to explain what was happening.

"This the same as happen to other men...all other men. That is why we are alone."

I believe he had tears in his eyes for our situation and the fact that they had been isolated from surrounding tribes for so long. Even though I was racked with pain and bordered on delirium, I had solved one of the mysteries of the Yall. Their gene pool had become a closed situation that would not be diluted by intermarriage with others. All others who came near them eventually died. Thus, the Caucasian strain (which I still couldn't explain) remained intact and passed on from generation to generation.

Our expedition doctor, Eduardo Gomez, was the next to pass. However, before his demise, he held my hand and apologized for not being able to solve the mystery of our illness.

"If only we had contacted my colleagues in civilization, we could have understood the problem. But, unfortunately, I didn't have enough equipment or knowledge to deal with it here."

I nodded. We knew the risks of having no radio or cellular phone contact with the outside world and were willing to take the gamble. Unfortunately, we lost.

"It has to be something that we all eat, drink, or breathe to which the Yall have developed an immunity. But, unfortunately, I couldn't figure out what it was in time."

I told him my theory of it being the *mommo*.

"You could be right..." Those were his last words.

At that moment, I decided that the three remaining members of our expedition would try to return to civilization. I doubted we could be successful but felt we had no other alternative. However, if all of Donald Colson's group had died and our group was heading in the same direction, we had no choice. We had to overcome our illness and fatigue.

Our departure saddened the Yall, but they understood. They had seen this happen too often—whether white explorers or local natives. They offered to supply our boat with food and water to make our journey possible. Because I theorized that the food or *mommo* was the main culprit, I asked only for pure water. They acceded to my wishes and took us as far as the waterfall. Some ancient legendary warning kept them from going further, so we bid them farewell.

I knew I did not need to make it all the way back to Manaus, Brazil. I just needed to get close enough to make radio contact. However, considering our state, that seemed a long shot. My only two compatriots alive were Hector Gonzalez, one of our native guides, and Leonard Groos, my long-time assistant. We took turns steering our motorized boat, but our weakening condition made every mile difficult. As the two of them were in worse shape than I was, I took longer and longer shifts at the steering wheel. My thirst grew intolerable, but I couldn't leave my task to imbibe. Yet I encouraged Hector and Leonard to drink as much as they could.

They had gone through two full jugs of water when they came upon the third, and I could see from their expression that something was wrong.

"*Mommo,*" whispered Hector.

"Don't drink it. Throw it overboard."

If they had the strength to lift it, they might have listened to my instruction. But instead, they merely marked it with an "X" and drank from the last of the two pure water jugs. I realized then that if I returned to the real world, I would have this jug tested and find out what was in it that was probably killing us.

Leonard died the next day, and Hector was fading fast when I finally made radio contact with the doctors in Manaus.

"They are almost all dead, and I am going fast. Please…help me."

"We have analyzed Colson's blood and know the cause of his death. However, the answer seems impossible, considering where he contracted this disease."

"Just tell me."

"It is usually found in poor urban areas where the infrastructure decays rapidly."

"What are you talking about?"

"Colson died of copper poisoning."

"The Yall had no copper pipes. They had no pipes or modern conveniences at all. There was no modern plumbing."

"Copper is found in nature. It is found in some plants like mushrooms, spinach, and cassava."

"We ate cassava. Is that it?"

"Probably not, if that was your only contact with copper. You would have to eat massive amounts for a long period. There would have to be another source."

"How do people most commonly contract copper poisoning?"

"When copper pipes get old, the water passing through them absorbs the copper. So every time they drink, they take in the copper into their systems, and eventually, it has an effect."

"Water…" I looked over at the jugs. "How would you know if the water was tainted with copper?"

"The water would be a deep shade of blue."

That was it. All the water the Yall ingested came from a stream that passed through a mountain that must contain copper. That beautiful tint to their water was deadly.

"What can I do? Is there any cure? Is it too late for us?" I yelled this as I looked at Hector, who appeared near the end.

"There is only one treatment that we know of. It has been used on sheep who suffer from sickness for years. However, it is quite rare. If you had the right ingredients, it could be prepared with sulfur and ammonium to create ammonium tetrathiomolybdate. However, I don't know where you would get the chemicals and the ability to combine them in your…."

"*Mommo!* Ammonium?"

"You're talking gibberish."

I wasn't listening to anything else they had to say. In some ancient times, someone, probably Redbird or Jack, had an agricultural or scientific background and had figured out that their only water source contained copper. They also knew the cure and synthesized it from available chemicals. The Yall of today didn't know anything but continued to put the *mommo* in their water. Outsiders, turned off by the taste, did not drink the water with *mommo*. Thus, they all perished. No one dared contact the Yall, and they remained isolated, forced to propagate a tribe with a unique genetic makeup.

I ignored the radio chatter and rushed to try and get the *mommo-*infused water into Hector. I was too late. As I raised the jug to his lips, he gave me one last sad look and passed away. I was alone. However, I now knew how to save myself. I quickly drank half of the "special water."

A few more days passed, and I did not feel much better. However, I was not getting any worse. As I downed the last of the water, I lay down and rested, content that I had done everything possible. That was the last thing I remember before seeing the rescue boat that would save my life.

⁓

Only the calendar on the wall made me aware of how long I lay in the hospital trying to recover. Physically, I was on the mend but still incapable of getting out of bed. However, my mind was working double time analyzing what I had learned and what I would do with that knowledge.

I had decided to destroy Colson's journal and any record of how to find the Yall. They were a happy, thriving population whose only suffering was brought about by the emotional trauma brought on by the arrival of strangers.

Yet my questions were still unanswered. Who was Redbird? Who was Nina? And who exactly were the Yall? As I became stronger, I started using my computer to look for answers. I researched everything I could about Percy Fawcett, and it was there that I found my first answer. I assumed that Percy died very soon after going missing. However, his son Jack did not. He had survived with one of the twin daughters. With her, he searched for a place to live and prosper...and found the Yall. How did I surmise this? Percy Fawcett's wife, Jack's mother, was named Nina. Would it be far-fetched to assume that Jack would name one of his daughters after his mother? My conclusion that Jack's daughter, Nina, was the "Mother of the Yall" was not a stretch. She had been half Caucasian. But for this gene pool to be so "White," Redbird and his son Fredbird also had to be Caucasian.

So, who was Fredbird...besides Nina's mate? Redbird had to be his father. He must have guided the two children until they reached maturity. But I knew nothing of him.

The question lay heavy on me. It was the key to the whole mystery of the Yall. What did I know? Redbird came down from the sky and traveled from the Brown Witch. It sounded all too B-movie-ish for my taste. And then the answer came to me from an angel of mercy—a nurse.

Angie (short for Angela—I wasn't kidding) was new to the hospital, having just arrived from America in an exchange program for nurses who wanted different experiences.

"And who have we got here?" Angie said enthusiastically upon first seeing me. Her energy and upbeat attitude were contagious.

"I am Dr. R..."

Yet before I could even get out my name, she interrupted.

"Wait, are you that famous explorer who went deep into the Amazon?"

"And almost died there," I answered.

"You were courageous."

"Stupid is more like it."

"I have only one question," she laughed out loud in anticipation of her query.

"Did you see Paul?"

"Huh?"

"It's just a story. One that everybody knows where I grew up."

I could use a good story to relax my weary brain and body.

"What I know to be true is the beginning of the story. How it ends is all conjecture...or you might say myth."

She told me a tale that I later verified to be true.

"So Paul was a great pilot by age 16, so much so that he gave up going to MIT to design and fly planes. He so admired Charles Lindbergh for flying across the Atlantic that he decided to try to outdo him and fly from our hometown to Rio de Janeiro. That distance would have beaten Lindbergh's trip and broken the record."

"And where was your hometown?"

"Brunswick, Georgia."

What? It was like I was struck by lightning. Brunswick...Brown Witch?

"Tell me more," I begged.

"He was spotted off the coast of South America by a Norwegian freighter and dropped a note from his plane asking them to point to the direction of land. The ship turned to point toward Venezuela. He was then seen by fishermen off the coast and others in towns and outposts near the Amazon. But he was never heard from again."

"This actually happened?" I asked in amazement.

"Oh, yeah, there were many reports of him being seen in the Amazon as late as 1935."

I thought to myself. This Paul guy was there at the same time as Jack Fawcett, and if he had a child, that child would be the same age as Nina...

"His father, Frederick, encouraged many search parties," continued Angie.

Frederick! I had to consider that Paul would have named his son after his father, Frederick. Frederick would then become "Fredbird" in the ensuing century. But there was no Paul mentioned in the legends. So, what was Paul's last name?

"Oh, I thought you knew of him? It was Paul...Paul Redfern."

Redfern...Redbird. All the pieces finally fell into place.

So Paul Redfern (Redbird) had flown from Brunswick (Brown Witch) and crashed into the Amazon jungle west of Matto Grosso. There, he had a child whom he named after his father, Frederick (Fredbird). Jack Fawcett had heard rumors of a "white man" and had sought him out with his daughter Nina. I supposed that Jack didn't survive very long because the Yall don't remember him. However, Frederick and Nina created their own tribe of white natives who spoke English. They kept their racial purity through no conscious effort but rather the tragedy of the blue water.

"I only have to figure out where the name Yall came from, and the story will be complete."

Angel started laughing hysterically, and I couldn't figure out why. Finally, she looked at me in disbelief.

"New York? Boston? Philly? You've got to be from one of those places."

"New York," I answered.

"I figured as much," she chuckled. "Any Southerner would know that a good ole boy like Paul Redfern would have greeted the first natives he came upon by saying. 'How you doin'…Y'all?' "

~

Story Behind the Story:

- In April 2023, I visited St. Simon Island, Georgia. There, I read the true story of Paul Redfern, who took off from a local airport and was never seen again. His last reported contact occurred off the coast of South America, heading inland. His father, Frederick Redfern, searched endlessly with no luck. It seems to me that every mystery needs to be solved—even if it is done in fiction.
- To this day, when people of St. Simon's Island meet someone from South America, they traditionally ask, "Have you seen Paul?"

PETE'S PLACE

⌘

The marker on the side of the highway read, "Darkness Falls – 2 miles." This information told me that this road had a destination—a direction. This sign provided some comfort because where I had come from remained a mystery to me. I remember very little about my past, and my definition of "past" is any event longer than three minutes ago. It was as if I had just been plucked from somewhere unknown and placed in this car on this road.

I knew my name was Isaac from an ornamental ID bracelet on my wrist. I believe I am eighteen years old (I am not positive of this because I can't recall seventeen years, three hundred sixty-four days, twenty-three hours, and fifty-seven minutes of that time.). I knew I had never seen the car I was now driving and probably could not even describe its exterior. I knew there was an old guitar case in the back seat and that I had memories of playing that instrument. However, any information beyond those facts eludes me.

As the two miles elapsed, I realized that the "exit" for Darkness Falls was not an exit—the entire road proceeded in that direction and that direction alone. Therefore, I had no choice but to move toward what I thought was a town. But maybe Darkness Falls referred to a waterfall, like Niagara Falls. I didn't know that either.

As the road curved to the right, visibility became impossible. It was oppressively dark, even though the sun had shined brightly only moments ago. I proceeded cautiously, with the car's headlights barely showing the immediate ten feet in front. I did this for what seemed like hours, but the clock on my dashboard only registered a few minutes. Then, I perceived brightness in the distance and drove toward it. When I reached the end of the dark (the darkness that fell?), I was stunned.

I don't know the technical term for what I was seeing. This area was the opposite of a plateau—an almost perfectly flat circular surface a thousand feet lower than the rim upon which I now rested, somewhat like a crater. The singular path down to the bottom was this road I was on. I then began to see a town.

~

As I drove by a large sign that read Darkness Falls, I could see an elaborate system of side streets that all branched off from one main thoroughfare that was dead center in the town. Someone had a sense of humor in naming this extra-wide paved boulevard "Earth Avenue."

I drove patiently, taking in the unusual sights around me. The road down the middle of town had three lanes with angled parking on each side. One lane went in each direction of the town, which was not uncommon. However, the lane in the middle went *only* into town. Giant arrows painted every ten feet told the driver to move forward. I would have thought this was some express lane for quick travel through the municipality, except that I could see in the distance that remaining on this path would take me right into the rock wall that made up the end of the valley. It was like the road was telling me, *go forward until you decide where to get off, but you must get off.*

There was no question about which side of the road to park. As I slowly traversed the town, a distinct pattern emerged. The left side of the road was depressing. The buildings were a ramshackle combination of poorly built and decaying structures. Indeed, from what I could see, even the people I passed seemed morose. They rambled onward, not seeming to be in any rush to arrive at any location. A gray hue hung over that side of the boulevard. This haze obstructed my ability to see what was going on accurately.

Meanwhile, the right side of the road was painted in brilliant colors, with every detail of its buildings in perfect condition. Few people were populating this side. However, those who were there displayed bright, engaging smiles. I moved from the center lane to the right lane and stopped a young man walking briskly down the street. He appeared to be someone right out of the 1950s, with greased-back curly blonde hair. However, he had a broad, friendly smile as he approached my car and looked in.

"Where can I get something to eat and drink in this town," I questioned.

He looked me over intensely, and then his eyes spotted the guitar case in the rear seat.

"You probably should be heading over to Pete's Place. It's just down the road. You'll like it there. Good food and drink…and a whole lot of shakin' goin' on…you know, music…real good music."

So, I took the guy's advice and soon found myself standing under a sign that read, "Pete's Place—A Beautiful Club Experience." That was a *weird description,* I thought. The building only had a thirty-foot, one-story exterior, so I didn't expect much. However, I was beginning to feel that I had gone insane when I passed through the front door and found myself in a vast concert hall—a much bigger space than the exterior implied.

There were three stages—one on each side and one on the rear wall. The place seemed filled, but as soon as I started to look for a place to sit, a table and chair became available right in front of me. I was starving, but no one came to my table. I felt frustrated as my hunger grew and finally stopped a passing patron.

"Is the service here always this bad," I complained.

He laughed. "You're new here."

"Yeah, just walked in the door."

"What would you like?"

"Why, are you the waiter?" He laughed at me again but apologized when he saw I was getting annoyed.

"I'm sorry. I forgot what it was like my first time here. Just think about what you would like, and you'll soon be taken care of."

"How do I know they have what I want?"

"They'll have what you want. So don't worry about anything. It will be taken care of."

"By you? Just tell me because I need to hit the head?"

"It's over there," he said, pointing to a corner.

When I had finished my business, I returned to the table. Sitting right before me was the exact order I had been thinking of…a well-done burger with melted cheddar cheese, bacon, and just the right amount of ketchup. Next to it were seasoned curly fries and an Arnold Palmer drink. What the heck?

When I looked over a few tables, the guy I talked to gave me a thumbs up. I had never said what I wanted to anyone. I should have questioned this whole series of events but didn't. I was too hungry. Besides, one of the stages had just come to life.

A young guy who looked like Chuck Berry was playing the guitar as beautifully as the original had. He even had his stage moves down as he crushed a version of "Roll Over Beethoven." He followed with a set of Berry's songs that were so good that I almost forgot how delicious my cheeseburger was.

When he finished his short set, the stage went dark, and to my surprise, another location lit up almost immediately. It was then that I realized that this club was set up as a place for tribute bands to hone their craft. The guy on this stage was doing Jim Croce material exceptionally well. I listened as he artfully performed "Operator," "Leroy Brown," and "Time in a Bottle." Then, that stage went blank, and the stage to my left became active.

I had always longed to attend a Chris Delaney and the Brotherhood Blues Band concert, but they were gone before my time. However, these guys were doing their hit, "Dancing on the Other Side of the Wind," just as I expected it would have sounded live from the originals. By now, I had finished my meal and ambled over to a crowd of people who were following the music from stage to stage. We now found ourselves at the first stage again.

"Those Born Free? I never heard of them." I questioned, and one of the girls answered.

"Not all great bands made it or were famous. However, here, we don't differentiate. Good music is good music…and good bands are good bands." She winked and then added something I didn't understand, "Good in every sense of the word."

They were good, and so were the three bands that followed. I had never heard of them either, but I enjoyed their performances immensely. The music had distracted me enough that I forgot where I was...and that I had no memory of anything before driving on the road toward Darkness Falls. Amazingly, I didn't care. The hours flew by, and I had a great time and worried about nothing.

I soon found out that the definition of good music was not limited to rock. At times, two stages were active, and by some miracle of acoustics, their sounds did not clash. If you were near one stage, you heard the music being played there, and if you drifted over to the other stage, that was the only sound you heard. The group of people I had started to hang with decided to educate me on different genres and expand my musical interests. I stood enchanted by some great jazz—a style I had never really given a chance. I was then introduced to a big band ensemble, and they told me it was Benny Goodman's style. I even listened to some Indian Bollywood stuff, followed by some mariachi from Mexico.

The most unusual style for my tastes was sitar music. I knew it was popular in the 1960s when the Beatles "discovered" Ravi Shankar in India and brought him back to the United Kingdom. They even used the instrument on some of their albums. But, as I stood appreciating the performance, one of the guys, I think his name was Johnny, started a conversation that made no sense to me.

"I sure hope we get to hear one or both of his daughters play here," declared Johnny excitedly. His girlfriend, Maria, sharply answered him.

"Why would you wish that? Sometimes, I think your head is up to your..."

"It's okay, Maria. I don't think he meant it that way. No one here would mean it that way," chuckled a friend called Gio.

I was baffled and had no idea what that conversation was about. I was about to make that point when another one of the group's friends, Jimmy Mac, called us over to another stage.

"Smokey Joe is about to perform," Jimmy Mac screamed to his friends. Talk about confusion. I was a big fan of Mississippi Delta Blues. My mentor, Southy Sam Layton, had told me stories of the

1930s blues greats and had me listen to some of his old records. But wait! I just realized that I remember something from my past. Southy Sam Layton had taught me to play the guitar from when I was ten years old to…? That I can't remember. I only know that he taught me well, and I spent many years with him. It didn't matter to either of us that Sam was white and I was black. He knew the blues as well as if he had been there himself. He told me he had learned everything about the guitar and life from an old black man named Fast Jesse.

In the waning years of his life, Fast Jesse had taken the young Sam under his wing and made him a professional musician who became rich and famous. The famous Southy Sam Layton had then returned to my little section of town to live out his final years. Besides using the wealth he had accumulated to help the poor of Southy, he taught me everything he knew. Included in that was the story of Smokey Joe. So now there was a young guy, perhaps in his late twenties, ready to do a tribute to this great but never famous blues musician.

If the *real* Smokey Joe Watson was half as good as his imitator, he should have been famous. He should have been rich and not have died penniless and alone, as Fast Jesse said he did. Instead, I listened to this "Smokey Joe" bend the strings and run his fingers over the frets with a skill that I could only dream of achieving. I stood entranced as his half-hour of playing time held me mesmerized.

When he was done, I asked my friends what his name was. Johnny, Jimmy Mac, Maria, and Gio were moving away from me.

"Sorry, we're on soon. Gotta go," yelled Johnny through the crowd, and then realized that they were the band Those Born Free I had heard playing earlier.

"But what's his name?"

"Joe," I thought I heard from Gio as he laughed.

Then, right behind me, I heard a voice.

"Smokey Joe Watson is my name, and I hear you is Isaac," spoke the young black man who had just been on the stage.

"No, what's your name really?"

"My momma done name me Joseph Watson, but that quickly become Joe. When I got older and developed a taste for tobacco, I soon became Smokey Joe."

"Cut the crap," I answered just a bit too quickly.

"You have no idea where you are or what's going on...do you?"

I didn't answer.

"I guess that's why my friends picked me to tell you the truth of the matter."

"What's that?"

"Let's talk outside...I need a smoke."

Now I thought he was staying in character—the whole "Smokey" Joe Watson image. However, when we got outside, he lit up an unfiltered Camel. He was committed to the image. I played along.

"Those things will kill you," I warned, and I have never heard somebody laugh so loudly. Apparently, I had said something funny.

"Robert Johnson used to say that to me."

Now I had him. This twenty-something is telling me that he knew Robert Johnson, the greatest blues guitarist of all time. However, Johnson had died in the 1930s. Honestly, I could not remember what year I was living at that moment, but I did remember that it was the 21st century. I also knew how to catch "Smokey Joe" in his lie.

My teacher and mentor, Southy Sam, had told me the true story of Robert Johnson. It had been passed on to him by his teacher/mentor, Fast Jesse, a friend and contemporary of the blues great. It was a story only the four of us knew. I would test this Smokey Joe wanna-be.

"Tell me the story," I insisted.

Smokey Joe took one final drag on his unfiltered cigarette, crushed it out on the floor, and began.

～

Robert Johnson and I played all the juke joints in the South during the 1930s. I was good, but he was the best. That wasn't always so. At first, he was just an okay kind of player and singer. He wasn't happy with that, so he did something that I would never do—he went down to the Crossroads. Now, we all knew who he would meet at those crossroads. But the rest of us never dared go there. Robert did.

He give his guitar to the devil, and when the devil give it back... well...Robert become the best guitar picker and singer of all. However, he paid a price—his soul.

"I know that legend. Many, many people do. It has been written about endlessly, and it makes a good story. However, only the real Smokey Joe would know the rest of the tale…the part he passed on to Fast Jesse and that Fast Jesse passed on to Southy Sam, who then passed on to me. If you are really Smokey Joe, you know what I am talking about."

"So you still ain't seein' the truth. Robert Johnson and Fast Jesse were both of my friends. I give Robert's guitar to Jesse because I worried about where it come from…you know…the devil man. Fast Jesse then give it to that white boy Southy Sam when he was ready to leave. And then Sam give it to…."

"You're stalling. If you are Smokey Joe, as you claim, you'll know the story that was told to Fast Jesse and Southy Sam…and me."

"You mean about Robert's last night on Earth and what he done told me? I guess you are testin' me."

"Yes, I am. Only the real Smokey Joe would know," I challenged him skeptically.

"Okay, you asked for it."

So, me and Robert are sittin' the bar takin' a break from playing. He suddenly takes my hand and says, "I just want to say goodbye." I ask him what he means, and he puts up his hand to stop me from talkin'.

"Let me tell you my story. I went down to the crossroads, and the devil give me all the skill in the whole wide world for the price of my soul."

"I know that," I interrupt.

"No, Smokey, you, and everyone else suspect that much, but you didn't know…at least not for sure. No, I'm telling you it's the truth, and I can't even say 'so help me God' because I give up that right after I made my deal."

"We have been friends for a long time," I say to him. "Why you be tellin' me this now?"

"Because that devil man is a tricky son-of-a-bitch. There be a part of the deal that no one know about but me. See, when he makes the deal, he sealed it with a tattoo that appear on my stomach. It's small—with just the number 333 right at my waist. It was his symbol for those he owned. His sign in the good book is 666, so those he own is 333."

"So what?" I ask him.

"So, I figure it's a ciphering thing. 3 time 3 time 3. That be 27—the age the devil man come for me."

My friend Robert died the next day…at age 27.

"Holy Shit, that was the story I knew, but how could you know?" I thought to myself. *The real Smoky Joe would be way over a hundred years old!* From his answer, I realized that he could read my mind. He answered my unspoken question.

"You stop counting years…when the darkness falls."

"Darkness falls, you mean that's just not the name of this town it's…"

"Would you like it better if the town was called…Kicked the Bucket…Pushing up Daisies…or…Taking a Dirt Nap?"

"You mean…"

"Yes, I do. Not only that, but the big man up there has a sense of humor. He is makin' fun of all those poor souls like Robert who made a deal with the devil. You see, all of us here in Pete's Place are in our '27-year-old bodies.' It's kinda nice."

"But then what is this place…exactly?" I was confused.

"I think it's pretty clear from the name." He pointed up toward the sign, "Pete's Place."

"Yeah, he likes to be called Pete…a bit less snobby than Saint…. you know."

I then looked up at the bottom sign, which I had read as "A Beautiful Club Experience" during daylight. However, I now saw that many letters were not lit up. The neon "u" was dulled. Half of the second "u" was gone, as was the "l." Only the "C" of the club appeared. The result was *"A Bea tifi C Experience*—A Beatific Experience."

I was having a hard time taking all this in when I remembered the rest of the Robert Johnson story. So many of the young music superstars had met a similar fate, dying at the same age. The media had sarcastically dubbed them the "27 Club" … Janis Joplin, Jimi Hendrix, Jim Morrison, Brian Jones, Amy Winehouse, Kurt Cobain—those are just ones the world knew. Had they gone down to the crossroads and made similar deals with the devil?

I forgot Smokey Joe could read my mind. He pointed across the street. It was the first time I recalled the drive into town that afternoon. I remembered the split in the road and how the two sides of "Earth Avenue" differed. As I looked over to the other side of the boulevard, the haze began to clear, and I could see the dilapidated buildings devoid of color or life. I could hear music coming out of one decrepit storefront. It was not exactly music; it was so out of tune that it hurt my ears to listen. I then looked at the sign next to the door across the street. I understood all that was to be understood.

Appearing Tonight
Janis Joplin with The Doors
Tomorrow Night
Jimi Hendrix with his special guest Robert Johnson

Just when I thought I had taken all this in, Smokey Joe pointed to the sign above the front door of that venue. My eyes followed his finger until they rested on the club's name, "Highway to Hell."

"Seen enough?" Smokey Joe uttered as he guided me back into Pete's Place.

"Is this some kind of entry place or something?"

"Yes and no. We all enter here to...well, you know where...but we are also free to come back and visit whenever we feel like it. So many of us do that a lot."

It's funny how I almost didn't notice that Smokey Joe had lost the unique backwoods drawl he had spoken with earlier. Again, reading my mind, he shrugged his shoulders at my thought.

"Here you can be whatever you want to be...and you don't have to pay for it with your soul."

I understood even though I was only eighteen (I think?) and had hardly lived. Smokey Joe again read my mind.

"Wait here a second," he ordered. He didn't explain but went to my car and took out my guitar case. Together, we reentered the club.

As I stood in the doorway, the entire club stood and cheered as if they had been waiting for me all day. The applause continued while I was led to the stage. I reached to take my guitar case from Smokey Joe, but he held it firm while someone came up from the side with a guitar in each hand.

"Would you prefer a Fender Stratocaster or a Gibson Les Paul?"

I grabbed the Strat as Smokey Joe walked off the stage clutching my guitar case, all the while smiling at me. Meanwhile, I found myself surrounded by a full band that looked like they knew what they were doing. Of course, they all looked 27 years old.

I was especially curious about the two guitarists who appeared on either side of me. They seemed vaguely familiar. One was black, and one was white. However, I was so excited that I didn't think much of it. My memory of music returned rapidly, and I played like I was possessed (wrong choice of words in this location?).

I played some Clapton and some Mississippi Delta blues that Southy Sam, my mentor, had taught me. I even remember playing a few songs that I remember writing and performing (and perhaps recording). But how did these two guitarists know these songs? They even took solos harmonically tuned to the solos that I was taking. This might have been the greatest moment of my life...or was it now the afterlife?

When I was done, I received thunderous applause. Sorry, there is no humility here—not after that moment. The two guitarists and I went and sat at a table. I had to know more about them. Smokey Joe joined us.

"How did you know what I was going to play?" I asked them.

"Hell, I might have taught you some of that," the white guy answered but did not elaborate.

"Jesse, would you explain? This kid is confused."

"Okay, here's the scoop. Me and Smokey Joe grow up together and was good friends—my best friend. The night before he passed away, he gave me his guitar. He says, 'I gotta go, you take this.' Then he says, 'You remember three things in life: You pray to God, you be good to your momma, and you take care of this guitar.' You have to understand that our mommas had also been good friends, but they had long since passed away. But we would always say to each other, 'Be good to your momma' meant be good to *all* people."

"And I did remember," whispered Jesse. "Yup, right until I give away the guitar to this young man," he chuckled as he slapped the young blonde sitting beside him on the shoulder. "I figure giving it to him was my way of taking care of it."

Fast Jesse looked at Smoky Joe and smiled, "We're looking good now, right?"

The two of them appeared as healthy, vibrant 27-year-olds, laughing and enjoying life, or should I say, the afterlife. But as I glimpsed once again at them for one brief moment, I saw Smokey Joe and Fast Jesse as the old men they must have been when he passed away. My face must have given away my shock.

"From the look you are giving me, you must have seen our 'old' selves. We do that every so often to remember how lucky we are. You'll see," commented Smokey Joe. However, Fast Jesse seemed impatient to continue the story.

"I didn't live that much longer after Smokey left me, but damn, I played the best guitar of my life. But I don't think it was just me. I felt that every time I played, my buddy was right there beside me...or better yet, in me. He was helping me to be better in every way."

"Just like a ghost in your guitar?" I blurted out. Where did I get that phrase, or what did it mean? I just knew it. I had heard it. I had lived it!

"Yes, that's just what it was like," recalled Fast Jesse.

Almost like a vision, I again saw Fast Jesse as an ancient guitarist. He was in a dilapidated old house with a young blonde guitarist who appeared to be around the age of 17. In my vision, the Fast Jesse was at the end of the road. He spoke in a broken, failing voice and struggled to remember the exact words Smokey Joe had said to him years before. He handed the young boy the guitar.

"I gotta go. You take this," uttered the rasping voice to the young blonde. I could see the faint image of Smokey Joe standing behind his friend Jesse, whispering in his ear.

"You remember three things: You pray to God. You be good to your momma, And you take care of this guitar."

The vision transformed into a scene of this young boy playing to a large crowd of adoring fans. Over his shoulder, I could see Fast Jesse smiling, almost urging on the performance...helping the young man play...just like the ghost in his guitar. But how did I know that phrase? And then the young man began to age before my eyes, and I understood. Southy Sam Layton, my teacher, mentor, and friend, was the young man sitting at the table with me. He smiled at me when he knew I finally understood. As tears rolled down my eyes, I hugged him with all my might. Memories of a few days ago when he had left me as a man well into his eighties returned to me. And then I mouthed the words he had said to me.

"I gotta go. You take this. You remember three things: You pray to God. You be good to your momma. You take care of this guitar."

I didn't see it then, but I now knew that Smokey Joe and Fast Jesse must have been looking over Southy Sam's shoulder.

I looked back at the three guitarists, who now had all returned to their youthful appearances. Southy Sam smiled, and our reunion was only broken by the words of Smokey Joe.

"It's time," he said, handing me my guitar case. I held it in my hands, realizing that this guitar had been played by all three of them, and whenever I lifted it in my arms, they would be with me. I couldn't wait to retake the stage. I placed the case on a table, unlocked the three latches, and lifted the cover.

The case was empty.

I looked at the three of them, and they simply smiled at me, saying nothing.

Memories of my life flooded back into my consciousness. I was twenty and playing on stage, and the crowd was cheering—Southy Sam's vision stood behind me, guiding me.

And then I was thirty-something, and the crowds were larger. They were singing along to my songs as if they had heard recorded versions. I felt the admiration of fans and, more importantly, the love of friends and family as the scenes rapidly changed.

My life progressed through all its beautiful moments—maybe some not so wonderful as I watched my wife pass away from cancer in her sixties. I was alone.

"Oh, she's here," uttered Southy Sam. "She just wanted you to understand this whole thing before she came down the stairway from...well, you know where...it made a good song for Led Zeppelin."

I couldn't wait. I remembered how lonely I had been at the end... until I met a boy named Jake. I took the twelve-year-old under my wing and taught him the guitar, and his family became my family in my final years.

And then I knew why the guitar was not in its case. It had never been in there while I was riding to Darkness Falls. Instead, I had followed the tradition laid down by Smokey Joe, Fast Jesse, and Southy Sam. And in my last act on the planet, I had told the young man...

"I gotta go. You take this. You remember three things: You pray to God. You be good to your momma. And you take care of this guitar."

And then...I had given the guitar to Jake.

~

The Story Behind the Story:

- At its heart, this tale is merely a whimsical look at a man's life and his final journey. However, if you have read my previous works, this story is so much more. There are guest appearances by characters who inhabit my four novels (*Band in the Wind, Sound of Redemption, Brotherhood of Forever*, and *The Other Side of the Wind*).
- Additionally, there are song references that only exist in *that* world.
- I had thought about releasing a novella with "Pete's Place" as the conclusion to three interwoven stories. While each is meant to be read independently, "Crossroads" and "Ghost in His Guitar" are interesting, but not necessarily prequels to this story. These stories appear in my first short book, *A Flamingo Under the Carousel*. Also, in my "Robert Johnson Obsession Club" is the story "The End" in *this* book.
- Many have found it fascinating to reread the story to see if they can distinguish the real people from the fictional characters, especially those described, but not named.
- Finally, please forgive my constant references to Robert Johnson's thoroughly documented story. I have always found it fascinating. Robert Johnson even promoted the legend himself, writing the song "Cross Road Blues,"

which Eric Clapton would eventually cover as "Crossroads."

PART III

WHAT A WONDERFUL WORLD

"…And I think to myself,
What a wonderful world."

- Louis Armstrong

WHAT A WONDERFUL WORLD

$\mathcal{S}$ ometimes, writing is inspired by a specific location. To quote the Beatles, "There are places I remember all my life." In this part of the book, particular cities were used to create stories that are true, partially true, not true, or almost true tales. Yet whether it is fiction, nonfiction, or almost fiction, where these stories happen is essential to their telling.

"From a Window: The Story of Phil" (London) – Background

- This tale reimagines an actual event that happened more than a century ago. Though the story is true, I did take some liberties with the conversations.
- First Published in ***London: Smoke, Blokes, and Jokes of Foggy Town*** anthology

"The End" (Paris) – Background

- One final night in Paris. One final night to complete a deal —a deal of a lifetime.
- First published in *Paris: Love, Loss, and Longing in the City of Lights* anthology.

"No Kabeesh" (Rome) – Background

- Sometimes, being lost is an adventure unto itself.
- First published in *Rome: Centuries of Stories of the Eternal City* anthology.

"The Bobblehead" (Milwaukee and New York) – Background

- How people act can be quite different depending on where they were brought up…at least from the point of view of a native New Yorker.
- Pending publication in *New York* anthology (2025)

"Not All Those Who Wander Are Lost" (America) – Background

- "We've all gone to look for America." – *Paul Simon*. Some travel without a suitcase and roam the United States searching for new sights and adventures.
- Pending Publication in *Travel Adventures* anthology (2025)

FROM A WINDOW: THE STORY OF PHIL

$\mathcal{E}$ven though tomorrow would be a big day, she still tiptoed into the bedroom to put her grandchildren to sleep. London was abuzz about the city's current athletic events, especially the upcoming race. With all her children involved in the festivities, Queen Alexandra had taken on the responsibility of amusing her grandchildren. She could have allowed one of an army of well-trained nannies to administer to them, at least for this one night. After all, she was the Queen of the United Kingdom.

"Please tell us the story again," asked Henry, who was 8-years-old.

"Again? Don't you ever grow tired of the same tale?"

"No," they answered in unison. Henry continued, "Especially since we shall see it actually happen tomorrow."

"Well, you are not really going to see it. Tomorrow is just a re-creation...a commemoration of the event," The Queen answered quite calmly, not having the nerve to tell them that there was a very strong possibility that security concerns might keep them from seeing anything at all. The least she could do would be to tell them the story again.

"Yes, grandmother, please tell us of Philepsi...Philoso....Phil...something," begged Olaf, the second youngest at five. Additionally,

English was not his first language—a product of his father's Norwegian birth.

"You know what, Olaf? In the story, we shall call him Phil this time," consented the Queen, also not a native English speaker.

Edward and George, the eldest two, laughed at the story's hero being called "Phil." However, they conceded that most of their younger cousins would never be able to pronounce the Greek legend's name, Pheidippides.

"Yeah, tell us about Phil, grandmother," mocked the two brothers, who would one day be kings of their country.

"Now, now, boys, if you are ever to rule, you must learn to have compassion for those who do not understand everything you do. Yes, love, compassion, and empathy are just as important as strength, intelligence, and leadership," scolded the Queen.

George smirked at this concept and turned to his brother Edward, who stood straight-faced. He did not react at first but then nodded to the older woman.

"I understand," was all Edward would say. Twenty-eight years later, he would abdicate the throne of England after less than a year—a choice made so that Edward could pursue the love of a woman who was unacceptable to English royalty.

"If we are all done with the fiddle-faddle, I will relate the story of Phil." She glanced at the two oldest with a look that challenged them to comment. George made a motion as if zipping his mouth shut. Edward laughed and then imitated him in response. Finally, all the grandchildren sat and listened to their grandmother, Queen Alexandra.

"So once upon a time," she began but was soon interrupted by Mary, who was eleven.

"Grandmother, I didn't know this was a fairy tale?"

"It is not. I'm sorry. Two-thousand-four hundred and eighteen years ago…. Is that better, Mary?"

"Yes, Grandmother."

"The people of Athens were engaged in a great war with the people of Persia. These two countries were neighbors, only separated by a small body of water. However, they had disputes that soon blossomed into a major conflict."

"That could never happen today," interrupted Mary. "This is the

20th century. We have learned better than to have giant wars that kill many people."

"Have we?" retorted her grandmother.

"Of course, there will be no great wars in Europe," said George confidently. "Someday, I will be the king of England…and Grandmother, you know that my cousins sit on the thrones of Germany, Norway, Romania, Russia, Greece, Sweden, and Spain. This is 1908, not the Dark Ages. We are all related to our great-grandmother, Queen Victoria."

"Well, sometimes quarrels among family can be the worst of all," responded the Queen.

"Really, Grandmother?" said George, who was now quite interested. "No country you mentioned could rival our power…except maybe Germany. And Willy…excuse me…Kaiser Wilhelm II is my first cousin and friend."

"A world war…what a ridiculous idea," added Edward.

"Well, I hope you are right," conceded the Queen. "And I hope these 1908 Olympics help bring us all together."

"Grandmother, can you please stop talking to George and Edward and tell us the story of Phil?" whined Henry, who was bored with all the political talk.

"Yes, I will do that presently, and I'll not have another word from you two young men," scolded the Queen, looking at George and Edward.

"In 490 BC, the Persians invaded Greece," started the Queen only to hear loud booing from the three youngest children.

"Those nasty Persians," added Mary.

"No, the Greeks had started it at Ionia, but that is another whole story," countered the Queen, losing patience. "Children, I want to finish this story before tomorrow morning, so please don't interrupt."

All went silent.

The two armies met on a great field called Marathon. The most significant part of the Greek army was from Athens, with smaller city-states helping out. However, the Persians vastly outnumbered them because their most important ally, Sparta, had yet to arrive at the battlefield. The army from Sparta would have doubled the size of the defending Greeks.

Pheidippedes…sorry, I mean Phil—was sent as a messenger to beseech the Spartans to come. He ran for two days to beg for their help. The Spartans, however, gave an excuse and never came.

Faced with overwhelming odds against them, the Greek general had to be intelligent in devising a battle plan to save the Athenians. First, he positioned his army behind soft, muddy swampland. As a result, the Persians could not ride their horses to attack, causing them to be on foot.

Then, General Miltiades ordered most of his soldiers to the flanks, the sides of the battlefield. The Persians attacked the middle of the army, thinking it was small. It was a trap. When they got close to the waiting Greeks, they were attacked from both sides and routed...that means beaten for you younger children.

The Persians retreated, and the Greeks followed them to their boats, killing many of them on the way.

"Ew," complained Mary, who found this part of the story disgusting.

"I tell you all this because I want you to remember that war is not only about glory and victory but also about death!"

"Grandmother, finish the story," screeched Henry.

"Yes, Grandmother. The next part is my favorite," mumbled Olaf, speaking hesitantly, not confident in his English.

While all this was going on, the citizens of Athens were terrified. If the Greek army were defeated, they knew the Persians would march to their city and slaughter them. So, they waited desperately for word of the battle. Then, finally, Miltiades summoned Phil.

"Please run as fast as possible and tell the people they are safe. They must know of our victory."

Still exhausted from his run to Sparta and back, Phil sacrificed all to get the message to Athens from the battlefield of Marathon. With little thought to his health, he ran as fast as possible for the 26 miles needed. Upon arriving in Athens, Phil announced to the people, "We won," and promptly died. He had given everything so that the people of the city could know they were safe.

Tomorrow, the Olympics commemorate the moment when one man sacrificed his life for so many others. The race is 26 miles, recognizing the distance from the battlefield of Marathon to the city of Athens. That is a good thing. Very few remember the details of that long-ago battle, but we all remember Phil's run.

"Oh, Grandmother, I cannot wait to see the race tomorrow," piped Mary, and all the children agreed.

How could she tell them that security concerns were being discussed at that very minute that would prevent the children from being at the start of the London Marathon?

∾

"But your majesty, there are reports of anarchists and perhaps a new group called Communists in the crowd that could do your family harm," argued the captain of the Royal Guard.

"I understand," replied King Edward VII, pondering the problem. "However, it would mean so much to the children...all of them...your heirs. They would see firsthand the commemoration of the sacrifice that a human being can make for his fellow man. Isn't this important for them if they are to be the world's leaders in the future?" questioned Queen Alexandra, sitting by her husband's side.

"Yes, but if they don't live long enough to be those leaders, what good is it?" answered the king.

The debate raged on in the early morning as the marathon runners prepared for their race, unaware of the machinations in Windsor Castle. They went through pre-race rituals to ensure finishing the grueling 26-mile test. However, ultimately, the race was different from what they expected. The Queen had found a solution.

As the runners approached the starting line, race officials notified them they needed to assemble .2 miles further down the road. This spot coincided with the exact location of the children's rooms in Windsor Castle. Now, the children could gaze from their windows with a birds-eye view of the starting line. Their grandmother, Queen Alexandra, had found a way to bring the race to them safely.

∾

The Olympic Committee made the standardization of events a priority that year. This allowed for a comparison of performances from Olympiad to Olympiad. Therefore, all marathons run anywhere in the world since the 1908 London Olympics have been precisely 26.2 miles.

~

Story Behind the Story:

- World War I broke out in 1914 (six years after the 1908 Olympics). It pitted George V of the United Kingdom (who had succeeded his father in Edward VII in 1910) against his first cousin, Kaiser Wilhelm II of Germany.
- Eight countries involved in the war were ruled by descendants of Queen Victoria…George and Wilhelm's great-grandmother and ruler of the United Kingdom from 1837 to 1903.

All in the Family - World War I

King George V---- United Kingdom (Victoria's grandson)
Kaiser Wilhelm II--------- Germany (Victoria's grandson)
Tsar Nicholas I - Russia (husband of Victoria's granddaughter, Alexandra)
King Haakon VII -------- Norway (husband of Victoria's granddaughter, Maud)
Ferdinand I --- Romania (husband of Victoria's granddaughter, Marie)
King Constantine I ------------- Greece (husband of Victoria's granddaughter, Sophia)
Crown Prince Gustaf Adolf - Sweden (husband of Victoria's granddaughter, Margaret)
King Alfonso XIII ---------------- Spain (husband of Victoria's granddaughter, Victoria Eugenie)

THE END

彩

*H*e sidled up to the bar and ordered the first of many drinks he would consume that night. He intended to spend the night alone, choosing not to be with his girlfriend Pam or anyone else. There was no joy in his attitude, merely resignation to his fate—a fate that had been determined four years before.

"James, another?" asked the bartender of the small tavern on the corner of Rue Beautrellis in central Paris.

"You know, Jean-Pierre, people don't ever call me James."

"Would you rather I call you Buddy or some other nickname you Americans are so fond of? We Parisiennes prefer the formality, or should I say the class of a proper Christian name."

"If that floats your boat, then call me James."

"So, James, what are your plans for tomorrow's holiday?"

"I didn't realize that you celebrated our holiday. How American of you, Jean-Pierre."

"Do not forget that you Americans would not be independent if we French did not help you with your quest. So, the 4th of July is very much our holiday too."

"Then you can have it. I give it to you. I couldn't care less. I am enjoying Paris and the freedom from the shitty laws that keep me tied down in America. If I lose my appeal there, I go to jail. Therefore, I will probably be here forever…and I mean that quite literally." An all-knowing smile came across James' face.

It was then that James viewed a suavely dressed elderly man from the corner of his eye. His neatly trimmed beard framed a face distinguished by piercing eyes. His three-piece black suit was in line with the 1971 Paris couture. His cane appeared to be a prop, used simply to add an air of importance to his movements. He worked his way to the bar, dismissing James' desire to wallow in solitude.

"Mind if I join you?"

"Yes, I do mind," whispered the young man, barely looking up from his fourth Jack Daniels.

"You didn't say that when we first met four years ago."

"I'd remember if I ever met someone like you."

"I don't always look the same—one of the skills I am particularly proud of having developed."

The younger man looked closely into the stranger's face, and he knew. In reality, he had known for at least eight months that this moment would come. Until then, he had convinced himself that their encounter four years prior had been a dream, an illusion, perhaps the result of a bad peyote trip. But recently, he had come to realize that it had happened.

Ten months ago, in September 1970, Jimi Hendrix had died of a drug overdose. James had been friends with the guitarist, and indeed, they shared something in common that few would ever know about. James had been a struggling lead singer of a little-known group when he met the extraordinary guitarist in Mississippi one night in 1967. They had gotten high together and gone down to a place Jimi only referred to as "The Crossroads." There, he had done the unthinkable—something that had not seemed real at the time. However, its reality had been proven time and time again in the last few years. Both he and Hendrix had made a deal with the devil for stardom. Unfortunately, the price had been their immortal souls.

Stardom had discovered him, and his unknown band became world-famous within months. Wealth and adoration followed. However, he rarely acknowledged the suspected supernatural origins of his success. He worried that something was amiss when Brian Jones, the leader of the Rolling Stones, died at 27 years old. And then, his friend Jimi died at 27. James had been to "The Crossroads" with his departed friend, and he had been made aware that Jones had been there earlier, thus resulting in the success of the Rolling Stones. It was Janis Joplin who had figured the whole thing out.

He had met the singer during a chance encounter years before and told her about his hallucination at "The Crossroads." Not having any personal success with her career, she had been interested. However, it was not until Hendrix's memorial service in September 1970 that James ran into Janis again. It was then that the two of them realized the truth.

The paparazzi recorded his altercation with Joplin. The public found it amusing that two great stars should have a violent confrontation over seemingly nothing. Unfortunately, those reporters were not privy to the conversation between the two.

"Janis, wait! We have to talk. Talk about…you know…about Jimi."

"It's too late, you idiot. You told me about 'The Crossroads,' and…. Well, what do you think is happening now? What do you think happened to Brian? To Jimi?"

"Yeah, but it could be years. Who knows?" She looked at him in disbelief. He didn't want to see the truth.

"You still don't get it. Brian Jones died at 27. Jimi died at 27. And goddammit, if we had done our research, we would have realized that the whole Crossroads thing started with the blues great, Robert Johnson, who spoke and even sang about going down to the Crossroads,…and he died at 27."

"You're just being hysterical."

"I'll show you who's being hysterical." Joplin took a bottle of Southern Comfort, smashed it over his head, and rode away.

Janis Joplin died three weeks after Jimi Hendrix in October of 1970 at age 27.

～

The sophisticated gentleman pointed to the young man.

"It's time. Would you like a little heroin to ease your journey, James?"

He shrugged his shoulders at the older man and finished his Jack Daniels.

The older gentleman giggled. "I just can't resist."

"Resist what?"

"The punchline."

"Punchline?"

"Come, James, it's time for me to light your fire."

∼

Story Behind the Story:

- James "Jim" Morrison's premature death in Paris remains obscured by mystery, rumor, and conspiracy theories about his demise. The death certificate stated heart failure, but no autopsy was ever performed. He was 27.
- Poets and artists are among the great and the good in Père Lachaise cemetery, where he was buried. Molière, Delacroix, Edith Piaf, and Morrison's personal idol, Oscar Wilde, all lie near the grave of the legendary singer of The Doors. Despite the legends surrounding him, Jim Morrison's final resting place remains the main tourist attraction of Pere Lachaise cemetery.

∼

And More:

- The above is a work of fiction. However, it is based on specific actual events.
- Jim Morrison died in Paris on July 3, 1971. This was exactly two years to the day after Brian Jones, founding member of the Rolling Stones, drowned in a pool at age 27.
- When Jim Morrison returned to America, he was facing jail in Miami for an indecent exposure conviction.

- Morrison spent his last day on Rue Beautrellis in central Paris.
- Though no one ever explained the reason for Jim Morrison's and Janis Joplin's altercation, it did happen. Joplin cracked a bottle of Southern Comfort over Morrison's head in a fit of drunken anger.
- Jimi Hendrix rose from relative obscurity, playing to a small club (Café Wha) audience in Greenwich Village to superstardom in a matter of months.
- Janis Joplin considered returning home to Texas because she failed to break into the music business before becoming her generation's most renowned female singer.
- The Doors toiled without economic or artistic success for two years before their first hit, "Light My Fire."
- Jimi Hendrix and Jim Morrison knew each other well.
- Thousands of people visit Jim Morrison's Paris grave each year.
- And finally, the timing of the deaths of so many musical artists at the exact age of 27 remains an unexplained coincidence. It has garnered significant ink from writers much more talented than me and is often called the "27 Club."

And still more –the 27 Club Membership Roll

The Board of Directors:

Robert Johnson (1938) – considered by many as the greatest blues guitarist of all time.
Brian Jones (1969) – guitarist and founder of the Rolling Stones
Jimi Hendrix (1970) – considered by many as the most original guitarist of the 1960s
Janis Joplin (1970) - Perhaps the most significant female singer of the 1960s
Jim Morrison (1971) - Lead singer of the Doors

Kurt Cobain (1994), founder, lead singer, and guitarist of Nirvana. Icon of "Grunge Rock."
Amy Winehouse (2011) - Award-winning British Pop/Blues singer

Other Members:

Rudy Lewis (1964) - Vocalist for the Drifters
Malcolm Hale (1968) – Founding member and lead guitarist for Spanky and Our Gang
Dickie Pride (1969) - British Rock and Roll singer
Alan "Blind Owl" Wilson (1970) – Lead singer of Canned Heat
Ron "Pigpen" McKernan (1973) – Founding member, keyboardist, singer of Grateful Dead
Pete Ham (1975) - lead vocalist of 1970s rock band Badfinger
And dozens of others from various genres of music.

NO KABEESH

"No Kabeesh," was my only response. It had been a long, long day. I realize that is not how the phrase is spelled or pronounced. However, what else could you expect from an (only) half-Italian American lost in Rome? Still, I was rude that night, and I knew it.

We had had a wonderful two weeks on one of those all-inclusive tours of Italy. Every stop along the way had proved exciting and informative. The cathedrals of Milan, the Leaning Tower of Pisa, and the Canals of Venice had only been a prelude to the conclusion of our tour in historic Rome. Perhaps the feeling that we did not want this trip to end made my wife and I take off on our own on our last night in the "Eternal City." It was only then that we realized that we had been systematically sheltered during our entire stay from the fact that we did not speak Italian.

Previously, every person we encountered spoke English. From the moment we disembarked in Milan to start our tour to that last night, there had never been a significant problem. Sometimes, it was a bit rough since our tour guide always thought we knew what he was talking about, even when his English pronunciations were way out there. For example, he went through a whole narration about the role of "Yipsies" in Italian culture. Was he referring to hippies, yippies, and some uniquely Italian cult that was found in the cities of Italy? Only after thirty of us looked at him dumbfounded did we realize he was referring to the Gypsy subculture that could be found mainly around Florence.

We had expected that our lack of knowledge of the native tongue could be a problem when we booked the tour. But we had two defenses against any difficulties that might occur. First, our daughter spoke the language and was with us as part of her college graduation gift. Secondly, we had both been brought up in Italian homes.

Our daughter's language skills had saved us on more than one occasion. I especially remember the time we stopped at a roadside fast-food restaurant. In Italy, these places serve what we in America would call a full pasta meal at a place that looks remarkably like a McDonald's hamburger location. It was unusual for our tour guide to leave us to fend for ourselves. It was only after we realized that this stop was in an area close to where the tour guide's latest flame lived that we understood. He had arranged a lunchtime rendezvous while poor me was trying to decipher the overhead offerings.

Without our daughter, who had slipped away to talk with some friends, my wife and I were on our own. There were five overhead boxes labeled with the numbers one to five, much like a Chinese restaurant at home. All I had to do was pick a number. Simple right? Not so when no one behind the counter spoke a word of English. Instead of figuring out how to say in Italian that we wanted *two* orders of number *five*, I held up my fingers to designate my desire. Seeing the server put out *five* plates, I realized my mistake. I was about to get five orders of number two, *calamari* or squid, a food I distinctly did not like.

As I tried to correct my mistake, the server smiled at me and continued to prepare the five orders of squid. It was only my daughter's belated intervention that averted catastrophe. The server was more receptive when my wife and daughter decided they wanted the *calamari*. I stuck with number five—spaghetti and meatballs.

My second imagined defense against not speaking the native tongue was that my wife and I had grown up in Italian homes. Lol! All we had ever learned were mispronounced slang and a whole lot of dirty words. I swear it wasn't our fault. When my family had huge holiday gatherings (two dozen or more), ultimately, it resulted in the adults telling long, humorous stories and jokes. My cousins and I listened attentively as the teller went through all the details that made the story enjoyable. This storytelling would all lead up to the final climactic line— at which time all the assembled relatives would laugh hysterically—except for my cousins and me. The punchline was always a little (or a lot) off-color *and delivered in Italian*. What? We were deprived of the reward after listening to the entire story in English. As they said in Brooklyn, "We wuz robbed!"

Of course, we had to know the meaning of these words long after we had forgotten the pretext of the joke. Of course, the versions we heard of these Italian words were bastardized varieties that no Italian living *on the boot* would recognize. Before the days of the internet, it took me weeks of research (i.e., talking to other Italian kids) to realize that "fangul" had come from "bafangul," which in Italy was "Vaffanculo" or "Fuck you" in English. All this is to say that my wife and I had no useful understanding of the Italian language when we found ourselves lost in Rome on the final night of our trip.

With the planned part of our schedule completed, the tour members were free to choose our activities. Some decided to taxi to a particular place of interest we had seen during the day, while some found excellent restaurants where they could devour a five-course meal. Some, like our daughter, just rested and relaxed at the hotel. My wife and I decided to leisurely stroll around our section of Rome.

We descended the Spanish Steps and threw three coins in the Trevi Fountain. Then, we enjoyed the ambiance of the buildings and the people and chowed down on the best gelato in the world.

It was late when we decided to head back to our hotel. The streets were empty, and we assumed we had retraced our path back to the hotel. Wrong. We soon found ourselves hopelessly lost. Being the stereotypical male, I kept telling my wife I knew how to find our way back. It was always just around the next corner...until it wasn't. Finally, in all humility, I decided to ask for help. We saw a couple who looked like locals sitting on a bench. I got an unexpected response when I approached them and told them we were lost.

"Non-capisce," was their answer as they looked at us quizzically. They were *too* local and spoke no English at all. I knew this from my brief research as a kid. They correctly said the phrase my New York relatives used frequently but pronounced, "No Kabeesh." When my relatives used it had the underlying current of, *boy, are you stupid for not understanding.* When this couple spoke the phrase, it was a sincere answer that they had no idea what I was saying.

Not surprisingly, we grew frustrated as two more individuals responded similarly. Confused about what to do next, we sat on a bench and tried to plan our next move. We were then approached by a couple a bit younger than us. They also looked confused and frustrated as they spoke to us.

"We're Americans, and we're lost. We keep asking people like you to help us, but none of them speak English. Do you?"

"No, Kabeesh," I answered. I had a smile on my face, but they couldn't see it in the semi-darkness. They turned to walk away just as my wife gave me a swift kick to the shins.

"Wait," I yelled to them. The good news is that we speak English. The bad news is that we are as lost as you. Asking us for help is like the blind leading the blind."

"Misery loves company," they said, laughing with us as we started to walk in no particular direction.

"So, you thought I was Italian. My grandparents are going to love you for saying that."

We walked along, joking and having a good time with our new friends—wondering if we would ever find our way back. We passed by half a dozen hotels that were not ours, and they were all starting to look alike.

"I guess it's only the Italians who deal with tourists who learn English," said Sherri, our new companion.

"I think you're right...." I started and then slapped my head so hard I almost gave myself a concussion. I had the solution, and it had been there right before us all night. "Every hotel we have passed by has a night clerk who deals with tourists all day. They are required to know English. All we have to do is walk into one of these hotels and ask for directions." We did, and it was so ridiculously simple that I was embarrassed to tell anyone the story.

Our daughter was already asleep when we arrived at our room, so we decided not to wake her. We only had a little time to talk with her in all the rush and confusion to get to the airport the following day. As we settled into our seats and began the transatlantic flight, Brittany opened the conversation by saying, "You guys were out late last night. I couldn't even wait up for you. What happened?"

I looked at my wife, and she let out a little giggle. I smiled at her, turned to my daughter, and said, "No Kabeesh."

~

Story Behind the Story:

- A 2007 Perillo Tour of Italy

THE BOBBLEHEAD

What is the typical New Yorker like? With so many variations of race, religion, and ethnicity, it would take significant research to answer that question. However, ask me that same question about the typical New York *sports* fan, and I will claim complete expertise…and then tell you the story of "The Bobblehead."

How Big Apple fans "root, root for the home team" is unique—no matter which home team it is. Additionally, that rooting can be positive…or negative. After all, they don't call it the "Bronx Cheer" for nothing! New Yorkers always become emotionally involved with their favorites—sometimes too much. That is perhaps my one qualm about New York fans—the habit of a fan claiming pseudo-ownership of a team. "*We* won last night." "Boy, that play *we* made last night." I'm sorry, you never donned the uniform…*you* didn't win the game. *You* didn't hit the home run or catch the fly ball. The team you root for did all that, and you can rejoice in it; however, you cannot claim ownership. Sorry for the slight diversion before getting on with the story of "The Bobblehead."

I am an enthusiastic, obsessive New York fan. So, of course, the next logical question would be, "Which team?" My response is unequivocal, "All of them." If you put a "NY" on your hat, helmet, or shirt, I am your fan for life. Do you see a problem here? If you don't, I'm guessing you don't really follow sports.

This interesting dilemma only exists in New York, Chicago, and Los Angeles, not coincidentally, the three largest cities in the United States. In baseball, each city has two teams. A common belief is that if you are a fan of one, you must hate the other. Sometimes, these disagreements result in physical confrontations. I once witnessed an all-out brawl at a Mets-Yankees game. I was so amused as I sat with my mixed group of Yankee and Met fans that I cannot remember who won the fight...or the game. I am still working my long-winded way to the story of "The Bobblehead."

I am a fan of both the Yankees and the Mets. I am told this is a delusional fantasy. Yet, my reasoning is solid. I was too young to remember when the traitorous Dodgers and Giants were local teams, and so I had none of the hatred for the Yankees instilled in me as a youth by an older generation of fans for those teams. Simply put, the Yankees were the only team in town when I discovered the wonderful game of baseball. Of course, it didn't hurt that they seemed to be winners every year—a kid's dream.

Then, the Mets were created in 1962. They were a Queens team, the county where I resided, and it seemed natural to become their fan. However, my Yankee-hating (ex-Dodger and Giant fans) told me it was impossible. I asked why. These two teams would never compete against each other because they were in different leagues. The only place that could happen would be in the World Series, and there was no chance of that happening soon. In their first year, the Mets set a record for losses (120) in a season—a feat that has not been duplicated in sixty years.

Eventually, baseball started interleague play, and I had a problem. How do you watch a game where you don't want either team to lose? Matters worsened when the two teams met in the 2000 World Series. Not only did it require a split allegiance, but it also almost led to divorce court. My wife is as much a baseball fan as I am. However, whereas I *lean* toward the Yankees, she *favors* the Mets. So, for the first time in the thirty-eight years of the Mets' existence, there was taunting and teasing within the Rostron household. I will try to avoid mentioning that the Yankees won that series four games to one. (I wrote that I would *try* not to mention it; I didn't say that I actually wouldn't mention it.)

This love of baseball by both my wife and I caused us to set out in retirement to see every baseball stadium in America. We couldn't always see one of our favorite home teams on these tours, but sometimes we did. We had just seen the Mets play in Philadelphia when we drove our motorhome to Cleveland to see an Indians – Twins game. While at that game, we looked at the scoreboard and noticed that the Mets were playing the final game of their series in Milwaukee the next day. We packed up the RV at midnight and headed to Wisconsin, hoping to arrive in time for the game. And that is where the tale of "The Bobblehead" begins.

After driving through the night and parking our RV in a campground, we barely had time to drive to the stadium in the SUV that we towed along with us. Imagine our surprise when we reached the ticket booth, and they explained that the game was sold out! How could that be? The Brewers were not in a pennant race. They were not a good team and had not sold out any other game that year. After we got entry with standing-room-only seats, we discovered a bizarre reason for the packed house: "Derrick Turnbow Bobblehead Night." What? Have you never heard of him? You are not alone. I have told this story to numerous devout baseball fans in the past twenty years, who have all displayed ignorance of this little-known relief pitcher. His claim to fame was that he had recorded saves in the first four games of that season—a feat never before or after achieved. This accomplishment meant a great deal to Milwaukee fans. Go figure.

We settled in to watch the game and mingled with the local fans. This was one of the reasons that we enjoyed our tour of the stadiums. Besides baseball games, we were interested in the food and beverage choices, the architecture of the stadium, and, most of all, the people. We found that standing increased our enjoyment and understanding of the Brewer crowd. They were friendly and welcoming to "the strangers from New York." We talked to many of them while the game proceeded. The Brewers were leading for most of the game, 3–0.

"So, what do you think?" One of our new friends asked.

Was he referring to the actual architecture of Miller Field, which had a spectacular retractable dome, or to the general experience of a game in Milwaukee? So I gave a very generic "very nice." One of the other guys was more specific.

"So, how does this compare to a game in New York?"

Again, I didn't want to seem obnoxious. However, my wife intervened and said, "It's different." You could hear the sound of a can of worms opening up.

"Different, how?" Can of worms alert.

"Just different, that's all," she said, but I knew that wouldn't float. So, it was time to pull the bandage off all at once.

"Okay, in New York, we yell all the time. We yell encouragement when we are losing and jeer at the opponent when we are winning."

"But we cheer, don't we?"

"You cheer when something happens. In New York, we cheer *to make it* happen. And we don't just cheer, we boo…a lot. And it is not always at the other team. So, if you are a New York player and are not performing as well as the fans expect, you will hear sustained chanting. Strike out in a key situation, and you won't be able to hear yourself think."

"That doesn't sound nice."

"Nothing is nice about us if you don't perform as well as we expect. Maybe it pushes them harder or keeps the weak at heart from ever coming to our town. Whatever it is, it creates great sports moments and winning teams."

"So, all you care about is winning?"

"Is there anything else? But seriously, even if we lose, we have a great time—one you can never forget."

"I still don't get it."

While all this conversation was going on, the Mets had narrowed the gap to 3-2. I saw the worry on their faces. Then, suddenly, that fear, that desperation, turned to joy. Derrick Turnbow was coming in the top of the ninth to save the game. Derrick Turnbow of the immortal bobblehead fame. Derrick Turnbull, whose bobblehead every ticketholder received upon entering the stadium that day. Derrick Turnbow, holder of the four straight saves at the opening of the season record. Surely, he would shut off the Mets and preserve the game for the adoring home fans.

Except he didn't. Paul LoDuca, the Mets catcher, hit a two-run homer on his first pitch. This hit put the Mets ahead on their way to an eventual 4 - 3 visiting team victory.

"That's too bad," was the general attitude of our newly made friends. A resignation to defeat without any recourse seemed inevitable to them. But, oh well, tomorrow's another day.

It was a perfect teaching moment.

"No, you can't be just disappointed that your team lost. You have to be angry… and let someone know it…loudly."

"We don't understand."

I looked at the Derrick Turnbow bobbleheads that each of us held.

"If this was New York and Derrick Turnbow had given up the winning home run on his bobblehead night, there would have been swift and fitting retribution for that one act of failure. There would have been consequences."

"Like what?"

"So, how many Brewer fans were here today?"

"About 33,000."

"In New York, 33,000 people would have opened those boxes holding the bobbleheads…33,000 would have taken out their bobbleheads… 33,000 would have ripped the heads off, and 33,000 would have thrown them out onto the field."

"Are you kidding? These are valuable collector items. They will be worth big money."

I didn't know then what they considered big money, but my point was falling on deaf ears. Finally, I saw a passing man wearing a hat with a New York logo and called out to him.

"Hey, Fella, if a player gave up the winning home run on his bobblehead night, what would we do in New York?"

I could not have gotten a timelier response if he had been a shill that I planted in the audience. He pantomimed, taking the figure out of the box, tearing its head off, and then throwing it like a hand grenade. He laughed and continued on his way to the exit. Do I know my New York sports fans or what?

I smiled and bid farewell to the very lovely people we had spent a wonderful day with. I know in my heart that I had used the bobblehead analogy to explain what a New York sports fan was like. Still, I don't think they got it.

However, our friends were right about one thing. Two weeks later, my wife and I sold our Derrick Turnbow collectible bobbleheads on eBay for $50 each. The bidding came from the Milwaukee area. It was perfect timing. Less than a year later, they became worthless when Turnbow was gone from major league baseball.

∾

Story Behind the Story:

- I would show you the bobblehead, but $50 is $50.

NOT ALL THOSE WHO WANDER
ARE LOST

*M*y wife and I will spend over one hundred days on vacation this year. We will not pack suitcases or wait in lines at airports. No, we have been proud RVers for over forty years (nineteen since retirement). This choice has allowed us to visit the 48 contiguous states, 150 national parks, all 30 major league baseball stadiums, two Canadian Provinces, and scores of quite unusual places.

Many people would eschew our method of travel, opting for first-class hotels with all the latest amenities. But we aren't suffering. Our children are fond of telling us *it isn't camping when you have four flat-screen TVs, central air conditioning, a residential-size refrigerator, and a washer and dryer.* Our unique mode of travel is not roughing it, and since retirement, we have journeyed on 47 major trips totaling 150,000 miles.

Sometimes, we wander with no destination or timetable. It gives us freedom that is seldom felt in a modern world where everything follows a schedule. The phrase "Not all those who wander are lost" is lifted from the J.R.R. Tolkien book *The Hobbit*, but it couldn't describe our lifestyle any better if we had created it ourselves. Though we have seen all the traditional tourist attractions (Yellowstone is our favorite), we often roam to out of our way locations to seek the weird and unusual. We love discovering places, attractions, and events off the beaten path.

Last winter, we took a "Polar Plunge." These rapidly growing phenomena involve participants jumping into the ocean *in February.* Usually, these are fundraisers for worthy causes; the one we participated in was no exception. We got our requisite "Polar Plunge 2023" tee shirt and readied to enter the churning seas. Did I forget to mention that we did this in Key West, and the water temps were in the 80s? Yes, this tongue-in-cheek party was great fun and raised bundles of money.

Did you ever go sledding without snow? The White Sands of Alamogordo, New Mexico, are composed of a superfine form of gypsum conducive to sledding down them. National Park officials even encourage this activity —with one caveat. White Sands is also a missile testing ground for the United States. Potential sledders must call in advance to ensure no tests are scheduled on the day they wish to come. A communication breakdown could prove quite exciting.

Our California excursion included all the staple tourist attractions of Yosemite: giant redwoods, the Golden Gate Bridge, the Pacific Coast Highway, Hollywood, and so much more. But how many people visit the site of the tragedy of the Donner Pass? Early pioneers became trapped there during a snowstorm and resorted to cannibalism to survive. It seemed the height of irony when we left this location… and immediately found ourselves in an all-you-can-eat buffet in Reno.

In Minnesota, we visited the controversial Kensington Runestone, a stone with ancient markings that claim its Viking writers were under attack and about to be wiped out by local natives. This event supposedly happened centuries before Columbus and other explorers "found" the New World. I don't know if it was real, but the locals have based their entire economy on its veracity. For my part, it gave new meaning to the Minnesota Vikings football team.

On the coast of Oregon, we visited the small town of Astoria, which presents many unique experiences. It is where Lewis and Clark arrived at the Pacific Ocean. Harbor seals by the score frolic in the bay across from tours of the house where the classic movie "Goonies" was filmed. Juxtaposed with this lively town, a few hours away is Mt. St. Helens and its tale of horror. The long ride up to view the crater includes views of the destruction this volcanic eruption wrought, giving visible proof of nature's power.

These are just a handful of the hundreds of incredible experiences we have enjoyed. I could go on and on about the mysterious Cahokia Mounds in Illinois or sitting in Wild Bill Hickok's "death" seat in Deadwood. Perhaps I could tell you about how two Buffalo fought each other with our jeep in the middle of Yellowstone or how we climbed an outside ladder of a cliff dwelling a thousand feet high in Mesa Verde. You may be interested in the underground city beneath Seattle or Roswell, New Mexico, a city whose streetlights are glass facsimiles of aliens.

If food is your thing, I could go on about Cincinnati's version of Chili, Native American flatbread, North Dakota's Pitchfork Barbeque, and Rocky Mountain oysters (which, as many know, are not shellfish).

Lest I give the impression that it all was wonderful, I could mention the locust swarm in Kansas and the four times we had to evacuate an area because of coming hurricanes on the East Coast or avoiding a tornado in Oklahoma. And there is so much more.

After four decades, I realized that traveling might get harder at some point. Therefore, we have also adopted a second slogan that I found on a tee shirt in a Smokey Mountain gift shop. *You don't stop having adventures because you get old...You get old because you stopped having adventures.*

~

Story Behind the Story:

- This brief piece merely scratches the surface of our experiences on the road. (2000 days - 150,000 miles).
- I may write a whole book about RVing across the country. Then again, I might be too busy actually doing it.

PART IV

FOR WHAT IT'S WORTH

"There's something happening here,
What it is, ain't exactly clear."

- Buffalo Springfield

FOR WHAT IT'S WORTH

❧

*I*n my first book of short works, I had a section entitled "I'd Love to Change the World." The title is a take-off of a favorite Ten Years After song. That section consisted of opinion pieces that I had written and published in the past. If I did the same in this book, it would simply be a rehash. Therefore, this section is different. There are some thinly disguised opinions about specific issues (nothing significant). Instead, this is a miscellaneous section of stories I could not fit into any other section of this book. All my efforts to "put a square peg in a round hole" failed, so what you see before fits the quote from above. "There's something happening here. What it is ain't exactly clear."

∾

"Heroes the Great: How Comic Books Changed My Life" – Background

- In 2023, I was asked by Red Penguin Books to edit a book of poetry with the concept of superheroes in the media. After some urging, the project was expanded to include fiction, nonfiction, poetry, artwork, and photography, all centered on the basic theme. In contemplating the prologue for that book, I realized that an early obsession with comic books colored my entire journey of creativity in writing. They made me a reader, a writer, an editor, and so much more. I genuinely believe this to be true.

- First published in **KAPOW** anthology (2023) (Prologue).

～

"The Holiday Committee" – Background

- I have a lifelong fascination with history. While teaching, I came to the very unscientific conclusion that students (and people in general) either love or hate the study of the past. There are very few fence-sitters when it comes to this subject. Therefore, I almost became obsessed with seeking out history's minutiae and trivia to spark interest in my charges. I believed I could win them over if I started a lesson with a good story. I collected boxes of useless but fascinating trivia, unknown facts, legends, and tall tales. These were good as lesson starters, good conversation, and to help with an occasional Jeopardy category.
- In the "Holiday Committee," I created a group of people charged with establishing holidays in a brand-new fictional country. What is the basis of each holiday? And should they copy what the rest of the world practices? I hope that you find this tale both entertaining and educational.
- First published in **Fairs, Feasts, and Fiestas** anthology (2024)

"Seeing Red: The Good, the Bad, and the Ugly" – Background

- Continuing my obsession with trivia, I once contemplated a book that would deal with sports—specifically, how teams came to have their nicknames. In the end, I found myself dedicating more and more of my writing time to fiction, both novels and short stories. However, a vast treasure trove of sports trivia resides in cardboard boxes in a designated room in my house. When I saw an ad for submissions to an anthology titled *Red*, I knew where to go for resource material. From bullfighting to baseball to football, red has a great deal of meaning to many.
- Pending publication in ***Red*** anthology (2025).

HEROES THE GREAT: HOW COMIC BOOKS CHANGED MY LIFE

❦

Comic books taught me to read.

I have no doubts about that unorthodox statement. I was eight years old when I picked up my first Superman comic and became obsessed with the entire cosmos of superheroes. I needed to know every facet of their origins, powers, and relationships. It lured me into a world I had never seen before—a world of imagination. But responsible for my reading skills?

For 35 years, I taught children how to read. I knew all the methods available for a child to reach the peak of their abilities. Yet, one indisputable fact emerged. The more children read, the better they became at it. Like every other skill in life, practice makes perfect. I realized that it had been the comics that had made me into a voracious reader. I concluded that as a teacher, I would not only teach reading in more traditional ways, but I would also find a way to give credit to my students for outside reading…any outside reading. This sometimes included non-traditional "textbooks"—like directions to the latest video game or a TV Guide. Magazines, Manga books, and comics were all in the realm of class credit. One student even developed a penchant for reading cereal boxes. The bottom line was that I was recreating what comics had done for me.

Comic books taught me to be creative.

I can still picture eight-year-old Billy springing off the backboard of his bed onto the mattress below. My blue pjs and red towel cape offered no protection from the impact. But I was a superhero saving the world from the likes of any number of villains. There was no time for worrying about painful injuries. However, I was more than just re-creating what I had read; I was trying to visualize new storylines. How could I expand on what professionals had presented, or better yet, how could I create new themes…even new superheroes?

At nine, I created Dartman. Armed with about ten darts, I roamed my bedroom, bringing the unholy to their knees. On a distant wall lay a dartboard that I would target at the designated "bad guy." However, Dartman didn't throw darts standing erect and aiming like in a barroom contest. No, he threw them while flying through the air, targeting a villain while avoiding the weapons speeding toward him. He threw them sidearm, underhand, and through his legs. Dartman eventually was defeated when the super-villains named Mom and Dad noticed innumerable holes in the walls. (Dartman wasn't very accurate!!!)

Comic books taught me to write and edit.

When I was eleven, Robert moved in three doors away from me. Though I had many friends in my Queens neighborhood, none shared my love of comics before he came along. We spent hours reliving our favorite stories or news of upcoming events. What new superhero would DC Comics create? What is this new company called Marvel, and how will they ever compete with DC?

Eventually, we came upon a comic fan magazine that combined information with a touch of original stories. At eleven, we decided we could do that. We spent hours culling rumors and information about upcoming comics for our gossip column. However, more than that, we created our own superheroes. I created Miracal Man (which my co-editor reminded me was misspelled). He was my editor, and I was his as we produced that fan magazine entitled "Heroes the Great." We thought we were creative by changing the order from "Great Heroes" to "Heroes the Great." We worked untold hours on our project. We then put a notice in the most famous comic fan magazine – "Alter Ego." We were ecstatic when we sold our first (and only copy) to a stranger who ordered by mail. We had to produce it by typing the whole magazine with carbon paper attached. Robert could actually type, so he took on the brunt of that task.

John Lennon once said, "Life is what happens while you are busy making plans." By fourteen, I began to be overwhelmed with many of the joys and burdens that consume teenagers. I was in an academic high school, playing on the baseball team and performing in a rock band around New York City. And then there were girls!

Often, I sat in my bedroom gazing at my comic book collection and longing for the simpler times that the comic books represented. But as the Beatles said, "O-Bla-di, O-Bla-da, Life goes on."

I never lost that love of reading, creating, or writing. I have published dozens of nonfiction articles and three dozen published short stories, most of which are in my short story compendium entitled *A Flamingo Under the Carousel*. In addition, that imagination that I owe entirely to my comic book journey created four novels (*Band in the Wind, Sound of Redemption, Brotherhood of Forever, and The Other Side of the Wind*). Though there are no superheroes in my books, there are innumerable references to people I believe acted with superhuman courage, loyalty, and empathy.

And Robert? We have kept in contact, and he contributed a fantastic nonfiction piece to the Kapow anthology that I edited. It was surreal to work with him again—sixty years after the original Heroes the Great. What goes around, comes around.

∿

Story Behind the Story:

- Please excuse my pedantic slant on this topic. Teachers never stop teaching…and education never takes a vacation.

THE HOLIDAY COMMITTEE (OR MAY WE BORROW YOUR SPECIAL DAYS?)

❦

THE HOLIDAY COMMITTEE
MEETING #1

"Do you know what happened on October 10, 1582?" the frustrated Minister of Antiquities asked.

"No. I'm guessing some obscure leader's birth or perhaps a great victory in battle? Besides, I don't care. That gobblygook is your forte," the equally frustrated Minister of Finance answered. "You know the accumulation of useless information is the reason for your hiring...no, excuse me...for you being appointed to your illustrious...and useless position."

"How about a little respect here? I don't put you down for your uselessness. Mr. Minister of Finance? Really? We live in a country where the king makes 100% of the decisions about everything."

"Yes, but I advise him about how to make those decisions correctly."

"Big whoop. The two of you make a mistake, and he'll take another billion out of his back pocket to cover your screw-up."

"So says the Minister of Antiquities for a country that is only eleven months old. Hell, I have toothpaste older than this country."

"Excuse me, but I was hired for my knowledge of *other* countries' histories. I understand that I could relate the entire history of *our* country on a postage stamp, but that's not why I am here."

"Let's see you do it."

"Do what?"

"Summarize our history?"

"If I must. However, we do need to get on to our task."

"*Our* history is the starting point for what we must do today."

"Hand me that paper, and let's see what you have."

In 2019, Joseph James Simpson won the largest lottery in United States history—over one billion dollars. He then went to a casino in Macau because none in America would cover a bet of one billion dollars on Stony Brook University to win the NCAA championship during March Madness. ~~*Of course, rumors were that he somehow used his money to rig the result. However, they were never proven.*~~

"Good thing you crossed out that last part. It was pure speculation, Correct?"

"Oh yeah, correct. I know who signs my paycheck."

So, with his trillion dollars, Joseph Simpson bought Little Ragged Island, the smallest island in the Bahamas, for 11 million, but only on the condition that he would be allowed to declare it a sovereign nation—the Kingdom of Matilda, so named for his mother.

COVID-19 hit in 2020, and this little island had more than enough people who wanted to emigrate there. So, with his trillions of dollars, King Joseph created the most modern location on the planet—moving sidewalks, a monorail, a hurricane-proof domed stadium for all sports, luxury apartments, and so much more.

"The people worked hard to make this country what it is…and now they need a break," the Minister of Finance interrupted. His name was Francis Letchworth Wallingford. It was not actually his name, but King Joseph had renamed all of his closest aides with names that sounded like they were British House of Lords members.

"And that's why we are here," answered Alistair Alexander Crowden, the Minister of Antiquities (again, not his real name—the king really could be a bit of a jerk!)

"Yes, we will decide on ten national holidays for the Kingdom of Matilda. I will provide the worldwide political and cultural context. By the way, Francis Letchworth Wallingford, may I call you Frank?"

"If I must have this abomination of a name, I prefer Wally. How about you?"

"You can call me Al…and please don't start singing."

"I don't get it."

"You know, the 1988 Paul Simon Grammy-winning song, 'You Can Call Me Al,'…get it?"

"I have no idea what you are talking about. Old songs…Old things mean nothing. Money is all that matters…um….Al?"

"Our work is cut out for us because holidays are about recognizing the past greatness of someone or something."

"Well, that's your expertise. But where do we start?"

"Well, first, we start with a calendar, Wally."

"We have calendars all over the place. What are you talking about, Al?"

"We are charged with starting something totally new. For example, we could use the Chinese, Muslim, or Jewish calendar…."

"Why on Earth would we do that? We are an island only a few hundred miles from America. Why not just use the Western civilization calendar most world countries accept?"

"Yes, but which one? The Julian would be interesting—quite groundbreaking in its use of solar calculating…but with the corrections of the Gregorian changes. So yeah, that would be neat."

"Al, you do realize that you are rambling nonsense to yourself. Please let me know what you are thinking. We have a job to do."

"Julius Caesar created the first modern solar calendar. He almost had astronomy down to a science, breaking the year into logical pieces. They created regular and leap years. It was extremely accurate for 45 BC. That was before politics got involved. Legend has it that Julius 'took' a day from February and added it to…can you guess?"

"No, I can't guess."

"July…get it? July, as in the month named after him."

"Oh, that's wrong in so many ways."

"Oh, it gets worse."

"How?"

"When Caesar's adopted son became emperor, he was not to be outdone by dear old adopted dad. So he took another day from

February, added it to the eighth month, and renamed it after himself, *Augustus* Caesar."

"So that's why February is so short on days."

"Yes and no. No January and February existed in the original calendar before Julius Caesar created his version. There were only ten months, and the year began in March. Therefore, February was the last month added, so it got no respect."

"So, when they made January 1 the first day of the year, everything worked out...right?"

"Well, not really. September, October, November, and December translate into the seventh, eighth, ninth, and tenth months in Latin. It was never changed even when they became the ninth, tenth, eleventh, and twelfth months."

"This is getting too complicated, and our job is creating holidays. So finish the story."

"Well, in a way, my story does end with a holiday decision."

"Huh?"

"Most of Western civilization accepted the calendar for over 1,500 years. However, many still celebrate the new year in March. In time, many New Year's celebrations took place the last week of March, making April the first full month of the year. This made no sense since January had been the first month of the year for all that time."

"So, what did they do?"

"Okay, remember my first question to you today? What happened on October 10, 1564? Therein lies the answer. You see, the Church was the only power in Europe that could tell everyone what to do with any amount of authority. They realized that not only was New Year's Day screwed up, but a slight error made by Julius Caesar was now multiplied by 1500 years had made the calendar stray from reality. The months were now happening in different seasons, and the calendar had ceased accurately measuring a year. To the Catholic Church, this was important because the first day of spring was happening in winter! This meant that all their holidays, especially Easter, were thrown off. So, they fixed it."

"How'd they do that?"

"They made scientific changes to the calendar, creating what we have today. They fiddled around with leap years and made it work."

"Then everything was perfect?"

"Well, no. They couldn't easily make up for mistakes of 1500 years, so...."

"So...don't leave me hanging here...what did they do?"

"What happened was October 10, 1582. That's just a tease. I could have asked what happened from October 5 through the 14 in 1582, and the answer would have been the same—nothing...absolutely nothing. The days didn't exist. The Church decreed that when you went to bed on Thursday, October 4, everyone would wake up on Friday, October 15."

"And I thought daylight savings was confusing."

"The second part is more to the point. New Year's was officially changed to January 1. However, many did not get the memo. After celebrating through the end of March, they were ready for the new year on April 1. Can you imagine what people thought of them? What do you think they called them when they ran in the streets celebrating?"

"Ha, ha, ha, ha, ha...April Fools!"

"You got it."

THE HOLIDAY COMMITTEE
MEETING #2

"Okay, Wally, our last meeting was fun, but we must make more progress. We agreed to follow the United States calendar and not have April Fools as a holiday."

"Right."

"Yeah, that's why I brought in my nephew, Jeremy. He's going to give us a fresh set of eyes."

"Why?"

"So that we settle on the national holidays before celebrating our centennial!"

"Alright, let's start with Washington and Lincoln holidays," offered Al.

"Who are they?" quickly responded Jeremy.

"Is he for real?" asked Al.

"Education is not what it used to be," exclaimed Wally, defending his nephew.

"You know our first president and our president during the Civil War," commented Al, obviously annoyed.

"Whose first president and what Civil War," smirked Jeremy, revealing that his comment had been tongue-in-cheek. "He was not the first president of Matilda. We never had a president, or for that matter, a Civil War!"

"Yes, I see," admitted the humbled Director of Antiquities.

"We are not America. Therefore, we do not have to recreate their version of society," stated Jeremy, who acted smugly in evaluating the situation.

"But you must realize that 95% of our population were American residents two years ago."

"From where?"

"What do you mean?"

"Well, if they came from the Northeast, they would expect to have Presidents Week off. If they were from the great Mid-west, they might expect either Washington's or Lincoln's only...."

"But...," interrupted Al. However, Jeremy continued.

"If they were from the Deep South, they were celebrating Robert E. Lee's birthday on January 19, almost until the end of the 20th century," persisted Jeremy.

"Okay, I give up. No presidents. In fact, we can do away with Fourth of July, Flag Day, Veterans Day, and Memorial Day," chimed in Wally, who, as Director of Finances, was looking to cut out the days that people were paid and didn't work.

"I don't think that's a good idea," offered Jeremy, and Al immediately agreed, though he was surprised that the twenty-something favored these four holidays.

"Wally, Veterans Day started as the celebration of the end of World War I on the eleventh hour, of the eleventh day, of the eleventh month in 1918. It then became a celebration of all veterans of the armed forces."

"But then what is Memorial Day?" questioned Jeremy, showing he was not such a no-it-all.

"Shame on you, young man. Memorial Day is solely for veterans *who died* while defending their country. Big difference," chided Al.

"But we have no veterans. We don't even have an army," contributed Wally, trying to sound intelligent.

"Maybe we don't have armed forces in Matilda, but we do have veterans. They may have served in America, Canada, Mexico, or elsewhere, but they did serve, and we should honor them. Not just because it is the right thing to do, but as a practical matter, we may need them if we ever have to fight an aggressive neighbor." Al seemed to grow angry at Wally, confirming to Jeremy that Al was a veteran. Jeremy had a solution.

"Okay, how about one holiday…Veterans Memorial Day,"

Al and Wally nodded in agreement.

"Great," pronounced Jeremy, "And we can get rid of all the rest."

"Whoa, kiddo, do you know who pays your salary?" Wally smiled.

"I'm not getting any salary," replied Jeremy to his uncle.

"Yeah, well, if you ever want to get a good job in this country, you better remember who decides what happens here," chided Wally, Director of Finances and chief worry-wart about everything concerning money. He watched his nephew's face light up and could almost see a light bulb over his head, and he had a great thought.

"Alright. See how you like these ideas. You must have the Fourth of July because people love fireworks. However, instead of celebrating America's independence from Britain, we celebrate 'Founding Day' when King Joseph bought the island from the Bahamas and created this new country."

"Great idea," remarked Al.

"Wait, I'm not done."

"Then, instead of Presidents' Day, Presidents' Week, or Washington, Lincoln, or even Lee's Birthday, how about we celebrate King Joseph's Birthday on March 1, his real birthday."

"I gotta say, nephew, ~~you have got a knack for kissing up to the boss~~…excuse me…please change that last statement to 'You understand the country's needs to honor his majesty.' "

"And Flag Day could be honoring our flag."

"~~Jeremy, now you have jumped the shark. Our flag is a picture of King Joseph on a blue background. That is too much.~~"

"~~Did you really say that, Uncle Wally?~~"

"Oops, strike that last statement. And replace it with, 'Matilda Flag Day sounds like a great idea. Let's see if we have room for it in our calendar when we are done.' "

"Now we must consider Martin Luther King Day, Juneteenth, and Columbus Day…or is it now Indigenous People's Day? As our resident historian, Al, what do you think?"

"This won't be easy. Jeremy, every one of those days in America was controversial when it was first suggested."

"But we're not in America. Isn't that what you always say to me, Uncle Wally?"

"But you also must remember that most of these people were Americans two years ago."

"Al, help us out here."

"It's getting late…near my nap time. You know we older guys need our forty winks in the afternoon. So let's pick this up tomorrow."

THE HOLIDAY COMMITTEE
MEETING #3

"I notice we have a guest," observed Al.

"Yes, this is my girlfriend, Lucy. I thought she could help with our discussions," beamed Jeremy.

"Okay, young lady, we discussed political holidays at our last meeting. So I've prepared a fact sheet for your perusal."

"For our what?"

"For you to look at! Is that simple enough, Jeremy? Kids, these days don't bother to study the dictionary," quipped Al.

"We're getting off track early," interrupted Wally. "What about Columbus?"

"In a sense, he is our real founder. His first known landing was somewhere here in the Bahamas. Perhaps, even on this very island. Wouldn't that make us feel special?" added the historian Al.

"That's fantastic. It's a story that connects our history and the history of the world. What could be better?" pronounced Wally.

"Columbus also led ultimately to biological globalization."

"Biological what?" bleated Jeremy.

"Globalization. It means plants and animals were transferred to places they had never been. For example, the Europeans brought horses, pigs, cattle, goats, and sheep to the New World," lectured Al.

"And rats," added Lucy, who spoke for the first time.

"Well, yeah, they stowed away on the ships, but that's to be expected," spoke Al nonchalantly.

"Is it?" answered Lucy angrily. "We didn't have rats, and now we do. So that's okay by you, Mr. Historian?"

"A small price to pay for all those other animals," replied Al.

"Who decided that it was a small price? Columbus? Or the Taino who were here first?"

Al didn't answer.

"Didn't the Europeans also give the New World wheat, rye, and barley?" chimed in Wally.

"Yes, we gave you back potatoes, sweet potatoes, tomatoes, peanuts, pumpkins, squashes, pineapples, and chili peppers. However, my favorite in the list is tobacco so that all of you colonizers could get cancer."

"Am I detecting a bit of animosity from you, Lucy?" grumbled Wally.

"A little? How observant of you, Wally," chuckled Al. "Alright, Lucy, Jeremy obviously brought you here for a reason. So let's hear it."

"My real name isn't Lucy. Like all you pompous asses, I took a new name when King Joseph took our island."

"Excuse me, Lucy, or whoever you are; he bought it fair and square from the Bahamian government," screeched Wally.

"And what right did they have to sell it to him?" scoffed Lucy.

"Wally, calm down. Let's hear what she has to say," interrupted Al. "Lucy, proceed."

"I took the name *Lukku-Cairi*, which is our name for our people, who were all the original people that Columbus came upon. And, you two bigshots left out the most important gifts that were brought to us…disease and slavery."

"An unfortunate turn of events," interjected Wally.

"Unfortunate? You idiot, you don't seem to understand. By 1600,

99% of the population had died of the diseases brought by Columbus and others."

"She's correct, Wally."

"And for those who didn't die right away, there was always the alternative of slavery. Columbus thought that my people made great enslaved people," scolded Lucy, but her anger rapidly turned to sadness.

"Wally, I think that we should table Columbus. He is already controversial in America. Why bring that animosity and trouble here." Al seemed to end the discussion, but Wally continued.

"~~I don't know if we can do that. I hear King Joseph's grandfather was Italian, and you know how temperamental the king can be.~~"

Al nodded to the recording secretary, and she immediately redacted Wally's statement and started to reword the statement when Lucy interrupted.

"~~In light of the massive genocide perpetrated on the native population, we are heartily recommending that any mention of Columbus be banned from the country of Matilda, which should, in reality, be named Lucayos or Lukka-Kairi.~~"

It was already crossed out by the time Al nodded at the secretary.

Jeremy changed the subject and bubbled, "How about Martin Luther King Day and Juneteenth? Can we approve those?"

"~~Yeah, we should do that to appease our black residents,~~" said Wally.

It was crossed out even before it was muttered. However, Al still felt he had to reprimand Wally.

"You really are a superb jerk. No, not just an average, run-of-the-mill jerk, but one above and beyond all others. I will explain the history of Martin Luther King Day and Juneteenth, and then we can make rational decisions...just as instructed."

"Martin Luther King fought for civil rights with a non-violent method reminiscent of Mohandas Gandhi. His actions and speeches inspired many and moved the country closer to equality. After his assassination in 1968, the lawmakers started considering making his birthday a national holiday."

"They waited until after he died to *even* think about it?" questioned Lucy. "What does that tell you?"

"That tells me that he gave the ultimate sacrifice, and therefore, it raised the level of his commitment," shot back Al. He immediately realized that it was a trap.

"What about the hundreds of thousands of native Tainos that gave their lives to the European explorers?"

Al just shrugged as if to agree with her.

"What about Juneteenth? I don't even really understand that one," interrupted Jeremy in an attempt to ease tensions. Al, the historian, was quick to answer.

"Juneteenth is tied to the story of enslaved Black people in Galveston, Texas, learning that they had been emancipated, close to two and a half years after the Emancipation Proclamation had formally been put into place. So, it commemorates the end of racial chattel slavery across the United States. It is also tied to that particular event, in a place where you still had people who were still living in bondage, even as the Emancipation Proclamation had technically emancipated them some two and a half years prior."

"~~Okay, let's get back on track. No one in our little country of Matilda has ever been enslaved…or, for that matter, enslaved a person. Therefore, it is unimportant~~," angrily interjected Wally.

"You are so wrong. Our population is made of so many people whose existence was affected," solemnly said Al.

"So there should be a Taino Day, too," smirked Lucy.

"And Lincoln!" howled Wally.

It was Jeremy who offered a compromise.

"What if…what if we just had a Great People Day? It could mean whatever anyone would want it to mean. Our citizens could celebrate who they thought important no matter which culture or history they thought most important."

"That's a great idea, Jeremy. If you want it to be Columbus Day, Martin Luther King Day, or…."

"Hatuey Day?" Lucy interrupted. "He was a Taíno leader and the first prominent freedom fighter of the Americas. On February 2, 1512, he died at the hands of the European invaders because he tried to organize resistance."

"Yeah, what she said," chimed in Jeremy.

"~~Jeremy, you're just trying to woo your girlfriend. What if someone~~ ~~wanted to celebrate Hitler or Ghengis Khan?~~" Wally expanded.

Al nodded to the secretary.

"Not again. Are you going to edit my comments all day?"

"No, Wally, only when you say stupid stuff. Which is quite a bit lately," scolded Al, and then he continued. "Jeremy, I think your idea is fantastic, and I would like to expand on it. How about we also add a Great Events Day?"

"I like it," stated Jeremy, and Lucy gave a half smile.

"It could be Juneteenth, Fourth of July, or Guy Fawkes Day."

"Who the heck is that?" remarked Wally.

"Oh, just a guy who tried to blow up Parliament and kill King James I in 1605. But that's the point, Wally. It's a big fireworks day in Great Britain because the plot was uncovered, and the king was saved. It may not mean anything to you, but there may be people in Matilda who would miss their fireworks on November 5."

Wally was silent but accepted the concept of Great Events Day.

"We are making progress. Let's summarize. Secretary, please read the holidays that we have."

"Great People Day, Great Event Day, Veterans Memorial Day, King Joseph's Day, Founding Day."

"Thank you…eh…I don't even know your name," remarked Al.

"Noel," answered the secretary.

"Now that's timely. Your name reminds me that we must discuss religious holidays at the next meeting."

The Holiday Committee
Meeting #4

Wally looked suspiciously at the sixteen-year-old girl who now sat at the table. However, before he could speak, Lucy answered his question.

"This is my half-sister Maggie."

"~~Okay, this is getting ridiculous. Now, there are going to be two of~~ ~~them on this committee. Add my lovesick nephew, and they will make~~

~~all the decisions. We'll all celebrate the Taino God...whatever his name is."~~

Noel crossed out the statement even before Al, Lucy, and Jeremy got to look at her.

"We Tainos believe in two main gods, Yucahu, the god of cassava, and Atabey, the mother of Yucahu and the goddess of fertility. But what's your point? Our gods mean less than yours?"

"I just think that this committee may not represent the real will of the people of Matilda because it does not represent its total population."

"It would have if...."

Al knew that she would reference the hundreds of thousands of Taino who were the original inhabitants of Little Ragged Island before it became the Kingdom of Matilda. However, he also knew one other thing that he now revealed to Wally.

"I invited Maggie here because I knew she was *not* like Lucy. She was raised in America and represents an alternative view—a younger view than her half-sister." Al looked to Wally, Lucy, and Jeremy, and they seemed to accept his rationale.

"Besides, I just came from a meeting with King Joseph. He wanted to know what we had come up with so far, and I told him. He was so pleased with our idea of Great Persons Day and Great Event Day that he instantly told me to add three religious holidays to the calendar," Al exhibited his satisfaction with the concession that he had gotten from the king.

"What three holidays?" asked Lucy skeptically.

"That's just it—any three that a person would like. If you are Christian, it could be Christmas and Easter. If you are Jewish, it could be Rosh Hosannah, Yom Kippur, or Purim," began Wally.

"The Muslims could have their Eid al-Fitr and Eid al-Adha," added Jeremy, looking to Lucy to see her reaction.

"You might not call it a holiday, and we don't have a name for it, but...."

"Go ahead," encouraged Al.

"For lack of a better word, many of us Taino observe a sort of Un-Thanksgiving. Taino women dance to the spirit of Hatuey and ask for an answer from the *Great Mystery*. By the time the Pilgrims landed on Plymouth Rock, our race had already been written off as not existing."

"What a downer," spoke Maggie for the first time. "Can't you ever let go? If you must wallow in the past, then create a 'Taino Day' and get the people to celebrate what was good about your...our...culture. I'll help you do it."

Lucy nodded.

"~~Whatever floats your boat~~," announced Wally to the disapproving stares of all the others.

"Okay, I think we're done here," announced Al, but Jeremy interrupted.

"Didn't you mention that we could have nine holidays? By my count, we only have eight."

"You're correct," agreed Al. "I just assumed that Thanksgiving would be the ninth. It is the most universally celebrated holiday in the USA."

"We're not in the USA," mumbled Lucy.

"And in light of what Lucy revealed, perhaps, it might not be a great idea for Matilda."

"We could have a fun holiday like Halloween...or Valentine's Day...," bubbled Maggie.

"Okay, Mr. Historian, let's hear what you have to say about that," smirked Wally.

"Well, Halloween is a perversion of the words All Hallows Eve. The first day of November was considered the feast of All Saints, or as it was then called, All Holy...or All Hallowed. The night before a holiday was also considered holy and celebrated."

"Like Christmas Eve," interrupted Jeremy.

"Yes, just like Christmas Eve. However, in ancient times, the Celtic people celebrated the same night as the night that 'the dark time of year' began. It was the end of the harvest, and they had to hope that they had enough food stored for the winter. This uncertainty led to the observation of the pagan ritual of Samhain. To not drive away the pagans they were trying to keep Christian, the priests allowed the holiday to be tied to All Saints Day. It encouraged people to bake 'soul cakes' for the lost souls who might not become saints. Poor people were given these cakes if they went door to door on 'Hallow Eve' thus beginning…."

"Trick or Treating," declared Jeremy.

"Well, there is more to it…but, yeah, in other countries, different ways of doing things added to the event's flavor," groused Wally. "But what you are saying is that this has a religious background…sort of. Therefore, it falls under religious choices. Let's move on."

"Bah, humbug," jeered Maggie.

"Wrong holiday," quipped Jeremy.

"Let's move on," repeated Wally.

"St. Valentine's Day celebrates an actual person who most Christian churches made a saint. However, it was never a national holiday anywhere," began Al.

"Okay, then we can get rid of St Valentine," said Wally.

"Maybe, but there is an interesting legend associated with Valentine."

"I want to hear it," chattered Maggie. "I love love."

"During the Roman Empire, the Emperor declared that soldiers were forbidden to marry because it was believed to make them soft. However, if a soldier wanted to marry, he knew that Valentine, a Christian priest, would secretly perform the ceremony for him and his loved one. Eventually, he was found out and executed by the Romans. Thus began the tradition of him being the Saint of Lovers."

"Great story, but what does it have to do with our task of creating holidays?" groused Wally.

"Well, it could be one of the people's choices for Great Persons Day," offered Jeremy.

"Yeah, I like stories of love," added Maggie.

"Me too," added Lucy, smiling for the first time in a long time.

"You two are disgusting little twerps!" barked Wally.

"How about this," mused Al: "St. Valentine's Day stays an option for those who want it, but we create a whole new holiday that reflects the love of St. Valentine's Day, the general feeling of gratitude of Thanksgiving, and the understanding of our diversity. We could call it Love, Appreciation, Thanks, and Enjoyment Day or the LATE holiday. It could be late in the year as a celebration of all we have accomplished socially, culturally, and economically."

"Yes, but it is too late in the year, and it would conflict with Christmas, which you know many are going to choose as a holiday," said Jeremy.

"And if you make it the third Thursday of November, it is just our version of Thanksgiving—and you know how my people feel about that," remarked Lucy.

"How about November 11? It could then replace Veterans Day, which has been moved to May as part of Veterans Memorial Day." Al, Jeremy, Lucy, and Maggie looked at a makeshift calendar they had created.

"It works," Jeremy was the first to announce.

"C'mon, Wally. What do you say we make it unanimous?" proposed Al as they all looked at the group's last member.

"Okay, I'm in…as long as you mention to the king how instrumental I was in creating this calendar of holidays."

"And as long as Noel remembers to redact all of your…hmmm… inappropriate comments," teased Jeremy.

Noel nodded.

"Hey, Noel," added Al with a smile, "Come join us for a toast. As our youngest Maggie, would you do the honor?"

They all held up their glasses of water as Maggie led them.

"To LATE Day…to love, appreciation, thanks, and hopefully some fine entertainment."

∾

Story Behind the Story:

- More of that trivia that I have compiled. "Waste not want not."

SEEING RED: THE GOOD, THE BAD, AND THE UGLY

The old cliché is that when we get angry, we *see* red. I don't buy it. I see red all the time, and I am basically a laid-back person. I can observe the fury in a *red*-faced person boiling with rage, but I can also see the beauty in a red rose, or maybe a candy apple red sports car. This leads me to believe that red, like every other rainbow color, can evoke many reactions depending upon the circumstances. But let's look at the original premise.

I have never seen a matador perform. In fact, I haven't even watched a bullfight on any form of media. Yet, many believe this is where the original concept of "seeing red" came from. The matador, with his elaborately colored costume, waves a huge red cape in front of a formerly peaceful bull, and it immediately enrages the poor animal. In the real world, the actual rage can be attributed to the fact that the bulls were physically and mentally tormented before the matador ever stepped foot in the arena. Spiked lances are stuck in them as a prelude to the matador using a sword to kill the victim. A red cape being waved is the least of the bull's problems. To finally end this fallacy, it must be understood that *bulls do not see color at all!*

To further exacerbate my ambivalence, I can look to the many quirky *red* stories from sports, politics, and culture. For example, the origin of the Cincinnati *Reds* and Boston *Red Sox*'s names harkens back to a simpler time in America when colors were just colors…or were they?

Professional baseball began in 1869 when the Cincinnati *Red* Stockings (named quite simply for the color of their socks…again, a simpler time.) became the first team ever to pay all its players. However, in 1876, the Red Stockings joined the newly-formed National League and changed their name to "Porkopolitans." Huh? It should be noted that owner Josiah Keck owned a sausage factory in metropolitan Cincinnati and sought tie-in advertising. For the most part, the fans "saw red," ignored the owner, and continued to call them the Red Stockings.

In 1881, the National League decided to ban the sale of beer during league baseball games. Did I say simpler times…no beer at ball games? Nevertheless, Keck continued to serve the beer and was promptly booted out of the league. However, in 1889, when the National League changed its mind about alcohol, Keck's former team, now under new ownership, dropped the absurd Porkopolitan label and returned to the Red Stocking name. Yet, they quickly officially shortened their name to the "Reds." It would have been nice for traditionalists if they had kept that name from 1889 to the present, but that wasn't to be.

Political considerations motivated Cincinnati to change its nickname from the "Reds" to "Redlegs" from 1944 to 1945 and again from 1954 to 1960. First, the team lengthened its name to distance itself from Stalinist Russia's Communists, often called "Reds." Then, when World War II ended, they returned to "Reds."

However, in 1954, when Senator Joe McCarthy's congressional hearings vehemently attacked what he perceived as subversive "Reds" (yes, Communists again) in the American government, Cincinnati again saw a problem. The subsequent "Red Scare" in the United States encouraged the franchise to again change its name from "Reds" to "Redlegs." Finally, when the controversy was long gone in 1960, they returned to their traditional name of Reds. Did the team really need to prove they weren't a hotbed of communism …and was a name change ever necessary?

It seemed as if a lack of creativity was in the DNA of baseball's early owners. The Boston team also used the name Red Stockings when Cincinnati was thrown out of the league for the whole beer thing. However, the franchise dropped the name in favor of the "Beaneaters" in 1883 but retained the red color on their uniform. Red Stockings may not have been creative, but "Beaneaters"...really? They kept the name for over two decades, while many fans informally still calling them the Red Stockings.

In 1907, when the Beaneaters' National League manager feared that the *red* dye from the team's socks would cause infections, the team removed their socks and, along with it, their Red Stocking heritage. Boston's other team (in the new American League) immediately seized the chance to "steal history." The team formerly known as the "Puritans" jumped at the opportunity to take the "Red Stockings" name and claim much of the glory of its crosstown rivals. However, even that was a strange tale.

A crusade led by Webster's Dictionary and the Spelling Simplification Board attempted to "Americanize" many English words. A blatant example of this was the word "stockings" was changed to "sox." This movement failed with the noted exceptions of the baseball teams in Boston and Chicago, who continue to use this unique spelling for the Boston *Red* Sox and the Chicago White Sox.

Next, we have the case of the St. Louis Cardinals. Before you think this story of *red* got off track, or worse yet...is for the birds. Let me explain. Throughout the 20th and 21st centuries, the team has been nicknamed the "Redbirds." However, ironically, a red bird has nothing to do with the origin of the "Cardinal" name.

For the latter part of the 19th century, the St. Louis baseball team played under various owners and in numerous leagues. However, through those years, they were called the Browns or Brown Stockings (but never Brown Sox—at least someone didn't listen to Webster's new dictionary). In 1899, new ownership changed the name to the "Perfectos." (Sometimes, owners can be downright stupid when they try to be creative.) However, the other change instituted involved accenting the uniforms with a bright red piping and using red sox... oops, red stockings. There were already many Red Sox/Stocking teams, so the franchise continued with the Perfectos appellation until...

The story goes that *St. Louis Republic* columnist Willie McHale overheard a fan in the stands call the new uniforms "a lovely shade of cardinal." As a result, McHale began referring to the team as the "Cardinals" in his newspaper columns. This struck a chord with fans. By the 1900 season, the nickname had fully caught on as a rival newspaper, the *St. Louis Post-Dispatch,* also began referring to the club as the "Cardinals." That year, the franchise officially changed its name from the Perfectos to the Cardinals. However, it wasn't until two decades later that a pair of actual cardinals appeared on the uniforms. This long delay leaves no doubt that the team was nicknamed after a *shade of red* rather than a cute pair of birds.

Not all discussions of *red* are pleasant. There is a dark side. At the center of one controversy is the Washington Football team, which a few years ago changed its name from the Redskins to the Commanders. There is little doubt that the former name was offensive to Native Americans. Therefore, why did it take so long? The answer lies in the insidious stubbornness with which fans cling to names and their traditions. It is incredible that in a survey of Washington *"Redskin"* fans, 80% thought that the name should *not* be changed. However, *none* of them would use the word in their daily lives. But where did this offensive nickname come from?

The first Native American encounters with Europeans involved the Beothuk tribe, which inhabited the forests and shores of Newfoundland in Canada. The Beothuks coated their bodies with red ochre (probably as a mosquito repellant). The settlers who had contact with them initiated the term "red men or red-skins."

According to the Smithsonian Institute, natives sometimes referred to themselves as red men to distinguish themselves from white men when making treaties. This is evident throughout the 18th and 19th centuries. So, when did things get ugly? Despite these early instances, Native Americans might say the term "redskin," or even "redmen," has always been offensive. Still, a review of history proves that as relations dissolved between natives and settlers, the rhetoric changed drastically. Author L. Frank Baum (the author of *The Wizard of Oz*) *celebrated* the Massacre at Wounded Knee and wrote, "The nobility of the Redskin is extinguished, and what few are left are a pack of whining curs who lick the hand that smites them."

In 1915, the poet Earl Emmons released *Redskin Rimes,* an extremely offensive book. Emmons makes his intentions clear in the introduction of the work: "Those persons who got their idea of the Indian from Mr. Cooper (James Fenimore Cooper, author of *The Last of the Mohicans*) have pictured him as an injured innocent. Those persons have acquired the wrong idea of the maroon brother." The book consists of a series of poems, songs, and speeches, each more odious than the last. Emmons' book was symbolic of the usage of the word "redskins" in the late 1800s and early 1900s, as the word went from being an identifying term to a derogatory slur.

Yet, some deal with the whole issue with humor. The Red Mesa High School (almost 100% Native American population) brags that it is the home of the Red Mesa Redskins football team. Their attitude is *that-we-can-do-it...but-you-can't.*

A North Dakota collegiate football team of Native Americans took the unique attitude of fighting fire with fire. They named themselves the "Fightin' Whities," with a mascot symbol of a white man in a suit with a briefcase.

In the end, red is just a color between orange and violet on the spectrum, and there is a rainbow of possibilities of what it can mean. What we do with that information and how we react makes the difference in us as people.

∽

Story Behind the Story:

- More of my fascination with trivia.

PART V

WORDS

"It's only words,
And words are all I have,
To steal your heart away."

- Bee Gees

WORDS

I never thought of myself as a poet...in fact, I still don't. However, as a teacher, I taught students about poetry's beauty for thirty years. I found that they often balked at accepting poetry as relevant to them in any way. To combat this, I compared it to their favorite song lyrics. I then asked them to write a song (with or without musical accompaniment).

It was an enjoyable experience as it ingrained to both teacher and students the beauty of words. Poetry and song lyrics share a common bond. *How* you say something is just as important as *what* you say. It remained a fun and exciting exercise in learning until I hung up my chalk (in the days before whiteboards) and retired from teaching.

However, this joint poetry/song lyric theory became a very different experience in my incarnation as a writer. The series of novels that I wrote revolved around a sixties garage band that seemed destined for stardom. I needed original songs that the band created during their journey to tell this tale.

"Thief of My Forever," "Gypsy Rose," and "If You Live" are just some of the songs created for the fictional band Those Born Free, which inhabits my four novels *Band in the Wind, Sound of Redemption, Brotherhood of Forever, and The Other Side of the Wind.*

Interestingly, once the lyrics of a song were created for fun, I sat with my guitar and created the music to accompany the lyrics in the novels. If you know me personally or have read any of the "Author's Notes" in my books, you know that I cannot sing a single note on key. Therefore, most of these songs remain untapped gems, locked deeply in the mind of its tone-depth creator.

Yet each song has its own story...and one has made its way into the light.

∾

"Thief / Thief of My Forever" - Background

- I sarcastically wrote above that most of my songs remain "untapped gems." "Thief of My Forever" is the exception. The history of this song is a short nonfiction piece in its own right. It has had four different incarnations of lyrics and appeared in three of my novels. It has also been sung by a Broadway performer, recorded in a studio, and featured in an award-winning Proof of Content short film. Here are the cliff notes of its history.

- In 1997, fifteen-year-old Brittany Rostron wrote a poem called "Thief of Always" for a high school English assignment. It was an honest description of an adolescent's coming of age and her fears of losing her childhood thoughts and dreams.

- In 2011, I was cleaning out an old closet in her room and came upon the poem. In the early stages of writing my novel, *Band in the Wind*, I saw the poem as the ideal material for a song written by the fictional group Those Born Free, the main characters of my book. Though faithful to the song's central premise, the lyrics (except for the chorus) were manipulated to fit the plot. The title was also changed from "Thief of Always" to "Thief of My Forever." The song is also referenced in follow-up novels, such as *The Sound of Redemption* and *Brotherhood of*

Forever. Subsequently, the novel *Band in the Wind* and its pivotal song have been read on four continents and all fifty states. But that was not the end of the story for "Thief."

- Before the book's publication in 2018, one chapter of *Band in the Wind* was turned into a short story titled "Pretty Flamingo." That short story was not only published by the Visible Ink organization but was chosen as one of a dozen to be read and performed on stage in New York City. The song "Thief of My Forever" was not in the short story or the stage production. However...

- Brittany Rostron, now a graduate of the Syracuse University Newhouse School of Film and T.V., decided to write a script based on that short story. Though quite different in its focus, this film was also titled "Pretty Flamingo." Though using the same main characters, this storyline deviated from the original "Pretty Flamingo" and the book *Band in the Wind*. In this story, the main character, Johnny Cipp, sings a song that is now titled "Thief." Again, some of the lyrics were changed to fit this story. However, the chorus and main sentiment of "Time" being a thief of dreams and possibilities in life remained. Brittany reworked the lyrics to fit her story, and I contributed some of the lyrics and the essential music.

- The script for "Pretty Flamingo" won acknowledgment and praise in ten Hollywood and New York film script competitions. In December 2022, filming began on a "Proof of Concept" version of the film. For those unfamiliar with that format, P.O.C. is a slice of the script professionally filmed to engender movie financiers' interest. The film "Pretty Flamingo" won the 2023 New York Long Island Film Festival in its category.

- In this ten-minute sample, "Thief" is sung acoustically by the Broadway actor Javier Ignacio in his role as Johnny Cipp. While the credits are rolling, a full studio version is presented by musical director Lou Giangrande.

- Alternate lyrics appear in the books *Band in the Wind*, *Sound of Redemption*, and *Brotherhood of Forever*. Also, a hybrid version of the poem exists in my book of short stories (and one poem) titled *A Flamingo Under the Carousel.*

Publishing History:

- *About Time: A Coming of Age Poetry Anthology* (2024)
- *Pretty Flamingo* film (2023)
    - ‣ Acoustic version – Javier Ignacio
    - ‣ Studio version – Lou Giangrande
- *A Flamingo Under the Carousel* anthology (2022)
- *Brotherhood of Forever* – novel (2020)
- *Sound of Redemption* – novel (2019)
- *Band In the Wind* – novel (2018)

Additionally….

- The version above is used in the 9-minute Proof of Concept film *Pretty Flamingo*. If you would prefer to watch the movie and *hear* "Thief" sung, go to www.PrettyFlamingoFilm.com
- For more info on Brittany Rostron, her film, and her non-profit organization F.A.C.E.S – **F**emale **A**rtistic **C**ommercial **E**ntrepreneur **S**upport, go to www.Femaleaces.org

∽

"I Never Dreamed of Batman" – Background

- In 2022, I saw a notice for submissions for a book of poems entitled *Kapow*. I usually stay clear of this genre, not considering it a strength. However, what made this book different was its theme—superheroes in the media. On this topic, I was not only well-versed, but some might say a fanatic. I will say no more because I thoroughly explained my devotion in a different location in this book titled "Heroes the Great." I ventured into unchartered territory. "I Never Dreamed of Batman" is the only time I wrote a poem without expectations of it ever becoming a song.
- In 2023, publisher Stephanie Larkin of Red Penguin Books asked me to edit this book. However, it was evident that there was minimal overlap between poets and superhero enthusiasts. Therefore, I requested that submissions be opened to all genres of creativity. Eventually, due to Stephanie's flexibility and foresight, *Kapow* came to include poetry, fiction, nonfiction, photography (from Comic Cons in two cities), and even an original illustration.
- Tucked in among all that good stuff is my original little poem, which reveals the truth about my love for comics and all forms of superhero media.
- First published in ***Kapow*** anthology (2023)

~

"Love Is a Battlefield: A Dialogue" – Background

This poem, "Love Is a Battlefield," originated as two separate "songs" in different novels. "Gypsy Rose" debuted in *Band in the Wind* and continued in the sequel, *Sound of Redemption*. In these novels, it is a significant breakthrough song based on the vision the protagonist of the book, Johnny Cipp, had of a character whose life had been destroyed by his progression into harder drugs. (Starting with the gateway high of the 1960s, the affordable Gypsy Rose wine.) This vision of Tony's character by Johnny Cipp reflects my real-life experience of watching the destruction of more than one life in 1960s Queens. The song itself is written from the first-person perspective. The core lyrics and basic melody were initiated by the sixteen-year-old perfectly sober version of myself. I recently discovered a fifty-year-old recording of the song taped during a long-forgotten jam session in 1966. I dusted it off and put the final touches on it in 2018—almost a half-century later.

"If You Live" debuted in the book *Brotherhood of Forever*. In this book, the fictional songwriter reflects on the ongoing love he has for a girl/woman in a destructive spiral of addiction. Upon seeing the tracks on her arms, he writes the heart-felt lines, "I could love you…if you live, but that doesn't seem to be."

In "Love Is a Battlefield" (The title is a takeoff of a Pat Benatar song), I combined the two poems/songs to create a dialogue between a drug-dependent man and the woman who loves him.

Publishing History:

- *Pending publication in **Voices in My Head** poetry anthology (2024)
- *Band in the Wind* (Gypsy Rose) – (2018)
- *Sound of Redemption* (Gypsy Rose) – (2019)
- *Brotherhood of Forever* (I Could Love You) – (2020)

Thief

By Brittany Rostron and William John Rostron

We were living lives of passion
Never wanting to go slow
Never thinking, 'bout tomorrow
Never choosing to say no

We had the promise of a dream
To keep our fates at bay
Then, then came the Thief
And took it all away

In time, Time takes everything
No memories to treasure.
How long will he steal from me
This Thief of my forever.

Savage delight at my plight
Smiling as he grimly reaps
His dance brings my denial
His laugh brings my defeat

How could we listen to our hearts
Forgiving all our sins
Now we'll forever be apart
Just a song in the wind

In time, Time takes everything
No memories to treasure.
How long will he steal from me
This Thief of my forever.

Look here, stiff frozen in fear
Of the man I've always been
Fear of what I'll never be
Fear I'll never win

My words are left unspoken
The new dawn brings no sun
In the darkness I lie broken
Silent and undone

In time, Time takes everything
No memories to treasure.
How long will he steal from me
This Thief of my forever
This Thief of my forever

I Never Dreamed of Batman

When I was young, I'd be…
Superman
Leaping buildings in a single bound

Sometimes, I mimicked…
Flash
The fastest man around

But I never dreamed of Batman

In my room, I imagined…
Spiderman
Climbing a wall

I envisioned…
Green Lantern
The brightest light of all

But I never dreamed of Batman

In fantasy…
The Human Torch
All consumed with fire

Or maybe…
Hawkman
If flying was my desire

But I never dreamed of Batman

Club in hand, I was…
Thor
With his Hammer of Power

Sometimes, I could be
Aquaman
But only in the shower

But I never dreamed of Batman

Able to change size…
Antman
Shrunk so small

Powerful and smart…
Iron Man
Avengers, he led them all

But I never dreamed of Batman

Whether DC or Marvel
I was always a fan

The superhero didn't matter…
But never Batman

Because I never dreamed of Batman

No…Batman was too human
No superpower theme
If I couldn't be really special
What good was having such a dream?

I

A Bottle of Gypsy Rose…His Story

Blew my mind,
On a bottle of Gypsy Rose,
And now I don't need no more,

Blew my mind,
On a six pack of brew
And now I don't need no more.

I'm thinkin' about givin' up,
I'm thinkin' about goin' straight,
I'm thinkin' about givin' up,
I'm thinking…maybe,
…it's too late,
…for me.

Blew my mind,
In a brown paper bag,
And now I don't need no more.

Blew my mind,
On some lazy grass,
And now I don't need no more.

I'm thinkin' about givin' up,
I'm thinkin' about goin' straight,
I'm thinkin' about givin' up,
I'm thinking…maybe,
…it's too late,
…for me.

Blew my mind,
In a white powder haze,
And now I don't need no more.

Blew my mind,
Ridin' that horse,
And now I don't need no more.

I blew my mind,
I blew my mind,
And now it ain't there,
…no more.

II

I Could Love You If You Live…Her Story

I could love you,
If you live.
But that doesn't seem to be.

I could love you,
I know it.
If only you could break free.

Lines down your arm,
Are doin' you harm,
They're killin' you and me.

I could love you,
If you live.
But that doesn't seem to be.

I could love you,
I know it.
If only you could break free.

It's fryin' your brain,
drivin' me insane.
And you're too blind to see.

I could love you,
If you live.
But that doesn't seem to be.

I could love you,
I know it.
If only you could break free.

Monkey got a hold,
Of your damn soul,
Chokin' at my heart too,
Hear my plea.

I don't think you see,
What our future could be,
But I'm not going down,
... all the way
...with you.

PART VI

LIVE LIKE YOU WERE DYING

"And I loved deeper
And I spoke sweeter
And I gave forgiveness I'd been denying
Someday, I hope you get the chance
To live like you were dying."

- Tim McGraw

LIVE LIKE YOU WERE DYING

Certain people might not want to read this part of the book, and that's okay because I certainly didn't want to write it.

If you have read any or all of my books, you know I have a recurrent theme of fiction, nonfiction, and almost fiction. That basically means that I use every thought, action, or idea I have ever seen or experienced to create works of both fiction and nonfiction. However, there has been one part of my life that I have shied away from—something I have kept locked in the vault of my mind. Even now, I am beating around the bush—stalling incessantly.

I have recurrent, incurable cancer. I have had it for fourteen years and owe my continued existence to a team of excellent doctors at Memorial Sloan-Kettering Cancer Center. Oh, don't worry. I am not going to pass away before I finish this book. My ongoing goal is to die *with* cancer, not *from* it.

I started my writing career at almost the exact time that they sent me home from the hospital after my first surgery. At that time, I decided that I wanted to write to escape thinking of my illness. Yet I soon found that my writing and cancer are inexplicably linked together. Huh? Let me explain.

As I have stated, my novel writing began with my rehabilitation. I found my storylines while obsessively walking and listening to music. The songs and their meanings fueled my creative juices and led to four novels. But the synchronicity of my writing and my cancer did not end there.

From 2010 to 2013, I was both writing my novel and temporarily cancer-free. Though the doctors had hopes that they had contained and removed all cancer cells from my body, they consistently informed me that the odds were against that being the case. Life became a waiting game—with testing every three months to measure whether the nefarious cells were still roaming free in my body. Each test proved negative. Meanwhile, I wrote.

My writing was initially meant as therapy. My stories were filled with nostalgia. The culture and music of the 1960s were used as the setting for a humorous and tragic tale that was fictional, but based on real-life experiences. It was fun…and that was all it was meant to be. I assumed my audience would eventually be those who shared those times with me. With that in mind, I sent the first copy to a high school and college friend with a decades-long writing career. At that time, he was editor-in-chief of a magazine. I thought he would be part of a limited audience that would enjoy my tale of coming of age (including some murder and mayhem) solely because of the nostalgia of our times.

On August 21, 2013, I received a phone call from him. His first words will remain with me forever, "You've got to publish this." I know the exact date of his call because one hour after hanging up, my oncologist called. The first recurrent cancer cells had been confirmed in my system. How can I explain that day? Some of the joy of my friend's call got me through the nightmare that my life became. My wife and family were very supportive, and I put negative thoughts aside. I laughed when someone mentioned that I was recreating the theme of Tim McGraw's song, "Live Like You Were Dying."

My wife and I continued our RV travels, which took us to every contiguous state and every major league baseball stadium. We wintered in Key West, spent the summer on Long Island beaches, and enjoyed the Fall in South Carolina. There were close family holidays, events, and vacations. I lived with the specter of what the future held but was determined to live life to the fullest. And I wrote.

For the next five years, I edited and re-edited the book (eventually determining that it was too long and splitting it into two books). I researched traditional, self-publishing, and hybrid publishing options. Yet I couldn't pull the trigger. Despite my friend's continued insistence, I lacked the confidence to put it out there. Then there was that whole synchronicity thing I mentioned before.

In the summer of 2017, my cancer treatments and writing efforts crossed paths again. I was made aware that the nationally renowned cancer center, Memorial Sloan-Kettering, offered a writing program. My first thoughts were that this was a cute little benefit of having a life-threatening disease. I was then informed that this was an organization almost a thousand strong. They published an anthology of members' works each year, picking the best eighty pieces from over five hundred submissions for the book.

I reworked one of the more amusing chapters of my book into a short story and submitted it. This entry was to be my personal litmus test. If they liked my short story, perhaps…just perhaps, I would put my book out there.

On December 18, 2017, I received notification that my short story, "Pretty Flamingo," was not only going to be in the anthology but was picked to be one of twelve that would be read and performed on a New York stage by actors from Broadway and film. This final push persuaded me to publish *Band in the Wind.*

On November 28, 2018, the first copies of that book arrived at my doorstep. I know the date because it was also the date that my oncologist informed me that my numbers were up, and I would begin chemical treatments within a few weeks. It seemed too much of a coincidence. However, I used the time of my confinement to finalize a sequel to *Band in the Wind* titled *Sound of Redemption.* I received my first copy in late April 2019—the same week I completed my treatments.

My health situation was good in 2020. Unfortunately, this was not true for the rest of the country…indeed, the rest of the world. *Brotherhood of Forever* (Book 3) was published in the darkest days of the Covid pandemic. Although I was cloistered due to being immunosuppressed, the most significant effect was on my inability to get out and publicize the third book. No one was going anywhere—especially a bookstore signing.

With the considerable time I was cooped up, I looked for other activities. I retaught myself the guitar, read a great deal, and started writing more short stories. Those short pieces that were accepted by various publishers were then included in this book, and its short story predecessor, *A Flamingo Under the Carousel.*

Regarding the guitar playing, you'll have to read the story, "Déjà vu All Over Again." My bout with extreme chemotherapy is described in the tale "Senseless"—hopefully with a light and humorous tone.

When all the short stories were written, all the books read, and the guitar mastered (lol), I still had free time in my forced imprisonment. My wife, Marilyn, suggested that I write another novel. Having completed a trilogy that, I believed I had told in its entirety, a tale of fictional people who had grown near and dear to me. I looked at her with confusion.

"You never did tell the story of Maria," she chided me. For those who have never read my novels, that does not have any meaning. However, for readers who have read them all, you know that this main character in my first book was left abandoned by her boyfriend, Johnny.

This opened a whole new world of possibilities for what she would have done with her life.

Thus, was born "The Other Side of the Wind." This fourth book was completed while I was in the throes of chemo. When I arrived home from my second to last excruciating treatment, there was the first copy of the book waiting for me. Writing had always taken away some of the pain and brightened my mood. Sometimes, real life is stranger than fiction. My cancer and my writing are inextricably tied together…and that doesn't bother me.

At one time, I thought I was writing with a *literal deadline,* but due to the miracles of modern medicine, I no longer contemplate that. For now, I will keep writing, traveling, and playing the guitar poorly. My wife and I will continue to jump in the RV and seek the sand and serenity of that perfect beach…whether it is in South Carolina, Key West, or Montauk.

∽

"Senseless" – Background

- During the darkest days of chemo, Greg Kachejian, artistic director of the Visible Ink Program of Memorial Sloan-Kettering Cancer Center, contacted me. Specific authors were asked to write about COVID-19 and cancer…and film themselves reading their creation. "Senseless" is precisely what it sounds like. At the time, I had partially lost use of all five of my senses. I filmed myself, and it was streamed on a nationwide MSKCC event. I have a copy of that moment of "stardom." I have *not* put it on my website because it is too reminiscent of the bad times. I will leave you to imagine the hood on my head to protect my bald pate, indeed, all surfaces of skin, from sunlight. Sunglasses protected my eyes, even indoors, because I lacked eyelashes and eyebrows to keep dust and light out. The mask on my face protected me from COVID-19 and every other microbe since my body contained no internal antibodies for protection. Yet, this story is not depressing but instead meant to be humorous and uplifting.

Publishing History:

- **Writers Digest 2022 Award Winner**
- **MSKCC Visible Ink Virtual Performance** — "Cancer and Coronavirus: Perspectives on the Pandemic" — November 28, 2021
- **Visible Ink XIII** (2021 – 2022) anthology
- *Here In the Now: An Anthology for the Soul (2023)*

∽

"Déjà vu All Over Again" – Background

- What goes around…comes around. I based a story on a real-life experience…and then I had a solution to a real problem based on that story.
- *Here in the Now* anthology (2023), It is included in a trilogy of tales titled "While My Guitar Gently Weeps."

SENSELESS

✦

Chemotherapy has knocked me senseless. Hyperbole? Nope. The treatments indeed took away all five of my senses, rendering me unable to write the books and short stories that I so enjoy working on. I think that I am handling the garden variety fatigue, pain, and hair loss with dignity and grace. (Oh, God, where did my beard go?) But the senses, that was a whole new ballgame.

The first loss I noticed was my hearing. I have always had a slight ringing in my ears because I tended to play and listen to very loud music. However, I was surprised when I looked out at the bird feeders on the side of our house and reflected on how very loud the tweeting and screeching was at that moment. Were these birds on steroids? When I moved into the house's interior and realized the sound had not dissipated, I understood that it was steroids—the massive amount coursing through my veins and exaggerating the ringing. Still, I think my wife is jealous that I can now hear birds—real or imagined—all day and night without interruption.

Next up on the hit list was the sense of taste. Gone! I only realized how bad it was when I looked at the box that a delicious-looking pepperoni pizza came in and knew that the cardboard picture of the slice would taste the same as the actual slice sitting before me. This was ironically compounded by the fact that I did NOT completely lose my sense of smell. This meant that I could smell how tempting the food was, but I couldn't taste it. I began to feel that someone up there was playing a joke on me. I was thrown a crumb when I realized my total hair loss meant no longer having to trim those obnoxious nose hairs.

However, my hair loss included eyelashes, nature's protection against the microscopic debris that chronically assaults the eyes. Very soon, the hot compresses, drops, and medication only provided certain periods of definitive sight. I developed a new empathy for those permanently visually impaired. Listening to the TV and guessing what was happening became a game I mostly lost.

I had just gotten used to my limited sight affecting my writing when I realized that I had lost the feeling in six of my fingertips, making using a keyboard difficult. A friend suggested that I use a voice-activated program to produce written work. I was having difficulty with painful mouth sores, so I held out trying that method. When I gave it a shot, my extreme Queens accent made the entire story appear as if it were written in a cross between Slovakia and Mongolia. But you are reading this, so I guess typing with four fingers works, even if it takes forever

Senseless, yes, that's me. Well, not actually. I can keep writing as long as I can retain the most important sense—my sense of humor.

Story Behind the Story:
 • Though I am very proud of this work, I would rather forget the times I lived through while writing it.

DEJA VU ALL OVER AGAIN

Oscar Wilde wrote that "Life imitates art." He disagreed with Aristotle's ancient proclamation that "Art imitates life." I will not argue with those historical men who are way above my pay grade, but I would add this disclaimer—both statements can be factual. I know because, in my life, they were.

While searching for an idea for a particular sequence in my first novel, *Band in the Wind*, I used my real-life experience to create the fictional drama for my main character, Johnny Cipp. In the book, the protagonist becomes a bass player in an up-and-coming band. But how could I explain the thought process of someone becoming a bass player? Unless you experience it, it is hard to understand why anyone would subjugate the stardom of being a guitar hero to pound bass notes in the background. So, to solve this dilemma, I used my real-life experiences.

In 1965, I was a decent guitar player. I was improving steadily and hoped to achieve so much more. How good could I get? I never found out. While playing on my high school baseball team, an errant pitch crushed my left hand. By the time I recovered, baseball had left me—more ironically, so had music. It became next to impossible to fit my now clumsy, damaged fingers onto the frets and strings of a guitar.

One day, while trying to solve my problem, I picked up a friend's bass guitar and found that the size and position of the strings made it relatively easy for me to play. More importantly, I truly enjoyed everything about this unique instrument and its role in a band. I found fulfillment with a successful group of like-minded musicians.

I had my answer. I merely copied my real-life saga into my novel. The character of Johnny Cipp suffered all I had dealt with identically as I had. Why wouldn't he? I created him. I could describe the pain my character experienced by simply retrieving my memories. I could relive the ritual of soaking my hands in buckets of ice after practicing for hours. The real-life tale of a guitar player who became a bass player after an injury in 1965 became the story of a fictional character named Johnny Cipp. It worked well in a whole trilogy of novels. But the story wasn't over.

Writing the books between 2010 and 2020 brought back so many memories that I became enamored with the idea of playing the guitar again. With the onset of the Covid quarantine, I had excessive free time. A half a century of healing had given me the ability I had lost so long ago. My skills grew as they had never been allowed during my teen years. My wife bought me a beautiful Fender Stratocaster guitar for Christmas, and the sound quality improved even more. I had rewritten *our* story…both Johnny Cipp's and mine.

In September of 2021, three tumors were found in my lungs. They represented the latest location of a cancer that I had been dealing with for more than a decade. The doctors advised that the only solution would be substantial doses of chemotherapy for more than six months.

I recovered…but as a side effect, I had lost the use of the tips of my fingers. Whether it was permanent or temporary was undetermined. I struggled extremely hard to regain the guitar skills I had only recently gained. Many chord changes were filled with clunkers. The more I became frustrated with playing, the more I looked for a way to move forward. I never realized my path was right before my eyes—on my bookshelf.

The solution of the past was also the key to my future. I bought myself a new bass guitar and, with a great deal of practice, regained the skills of my youth. I reveled in my ability to lay down the bass tracks for Cream's "Badge" and the Animals' "We Gotta Get Out of This

Place." I had come full circle. I had taught my fictional friend Johnny Cipp how to cope with adversity... and now he had taught me.

As Yogi Berra had once said and John Fogerty sang in a song... it was like "Déjà vu all over again."

Story Behind the Story:

- You can't make this stuff up. Truth can be stranger than fiction.

AUTHOR'S NOTE

JUST A SONG BEFORE I GO

Those who have read one or more of my books know that I traditionally reveal fact and fiction in my writing in this last section titled "Just a Song Before I Go." I may have already overloaded readers with that background information in this book's "Introductions" and "The Story Behind the Story" sections. Therefore, I will make this a more traditional "thank you to those who deserve it" author's note.

- Thank you to my loving and precious wife of 52 years, **Marilyn**. If you don't know why I wrote that, you must have skipped over what I lived through in the "Senseless" and "Déjà vu" stories.
- This also goes for the rest of my immediate family, who are not just supportive but a whole lot of fun to be around: Justin, Heather, Samantha, Jarrod, Erin, William, Bella-Capri, Brittany, Mike, and Ava Marie…and of course "Crazy Alice"… "Mad Max"…and "T-Rex, the Bunny."

Thanks to:

- **Greg Kachejian,** Visible Ink Creative Director, and the force behind the five films displaying my work. These may be viewed on YouTube and my website. www.WilliamJohnRostron.com:

- **"Pretty Flamingo"** – Live performance videotaped at the Danny Kaye Theater (New York City - March 2018)
- **"In the Garden of Eden"** – Live performance videotaped at the Danny Kaye Theater New York City - March 2019)
- **"Ava's Bubble"** – Short film featuring Tony and Emmy nominee Victor Garber (2020)
- **"Fool On the Hill"** – a short film featuring film and TV actor, Jonas Cohen.
- **"The Last Chord"** – a short film starring film and TV actor, Ken Land.

- **Keyan Kaplan,** - My Visible Ink mentor and advisor who has reviewed and given advice on many of these short pieces.
- **Stephanie Larkin** – Head "Penguin" at Red Penguin Books for always taking care of my problems related to editing, formatting, and just about everything else. A special shout-out for allowing me the honor of editing the *Kapow* anthology.
- **Long Island Authors Group** – for the support, information, and camaraderie provided.

Coming Next…

Dancing with the Lost
A Novel

(May be read as book five of Band in the Wind series or as a stand-alone novel)

REVIEWS

A FLAMINGO UNDER THE CAROUSEL

"Rostron's writing remains addictive with great emotional engagement for the reader." - *Online Book Club Review*

"In all cases, dashes of life lure you into your own allusions and a sort of partnership of conclusions." *James J. Spina, editor of 20/20 magazine*

"Sad, funny, heartwarming. Everything wrapped into one." – *Amazon Review*

～

THE BAND IN THE WIND TRILOGY

"The *Band in the Wind* trilogy that is as staggering as it is entertaining!" – *James J. Spina (contributor to Rolling Stone, Hit Parader, Creem, and Mojo)*

BAND IN THE WIND

"This book is almost that perfect blend of music, nostalgia, a coming-of-age story...and tragedy! It really does have a bit of everything. Highly entertaining." - *Online Book Club Review – # 1 - 4/4 stars*

"This book is a must-read for book-lovers hoping to experience the lost, yet somehow lingering, days of 1960s American culture." *Michael L. Burduck, - Professor of English - Tennessee Tech University*

"This is a deeply moving, suspenseful, and mesmerizing book. - *Online Book Club Review # 2 - 4 / 4 Stars*

"This tale told by Rostron succeeds…massively. It is a story told with dollops of nitty and gritty and some blasts and burns that will thrill you as powerfully as…well…as a power chord. A giant power chord, amped up with emotions, friendship, cruelty, hate, revenge and love." - *James J. Spina (contributor to Rolling Stone, Hit Parader, Creem, and Mojo)*

"This novel really rocks! Rostron brilliantly evokes the time (The 60s), the place (Cambria Heights, Queens, NY), and most importantly, the music. Most novels about Rock and Roll are filled with clichés that just ring hollow, but this book just gets it right. The author really knows his music and really knows how to use it to set the tone." – *DSPIN - formerly of MTV*

SOUND OF REDEMPTION

"*Sound of Redemption* hits all the right notes, ringing true to the feel of *Band in the Wind*. Rostron's quirky sense of humor, reflected in the dialogue between characters, lightened the mood of an otherwise serious story. His writing is addictive, with great emotional engagement for the reader. This novel is a tense, moving, character-driven tale, exploring one man's mission to atone for the wrongs of the past." – *Online Book Club*

BROTHERHOOD OF FOREVER

"While you are in for a treat with *Band in the Wind* and *Sound of Redemption*, it is the *Brotherhood of Forever* that wins the Prize! Rostron is the master when it comes to portraying the tone and temper of a generational trek." – *James J. Spina*

"Rostron's *Brotherhood of Forever*, the third book of the *Band in the Wind* trilogy, masterfully rounds out his characters' lives in poignant, convincing, inspiring, and triumphant fashion." – *Mike Burduck, Dept of English, Tennessee Tech University*

THE OTHER SIDE OF THE WIND

"*The Other Side of the Wind* is another hit. It can stand alone or be read as the fourth book of the Band in the Wind series." – Amazon Review

"Another must-read for book lovers hoping to experience the lost, yet lingering days of 1960s American music and culture." – M. Burduck, professor of English. Tennessee Tech University.

"An extremely engaging book that kept me hooked. I do believe this book has everything it takes for it to be a *Bestseller!* "– Katherine Abraham, author of *Sunset Has a Story*

ABOUT THE AUTHOR

William John Rostron's books have a readership that spans four continents and all fifty states. His series of novels steeped in 1960s music and culture (*Band in the Wind, Sound of Redemption, Brotherhood of Forever,* and *The Other Side of the Wind*) have received critical acclaim from *Writers Digest,* the Online Book Club Review, and have consistently received Amazon ratings of 4.5 out of 5 or higher. He has published over three dozen short stories in anthologies, with five receiving awards from *Writers Digest* in 2022. Many of these pieces appear in his short story compilations, *A Flamingo Under the Carousel* and *T-Rex Stole My Computer.* Additionally, five of his stories have been produced on the New York stage or have been made into short films. Viewing is available on the author's website. Recently, he was executive producer for the short film "Pretty Flamingo" which was based on his short story of the same name. This film, scripted by his daughter, Brittany Rostron, took first place in its category in the New York Long Island Film Festival.

Born and raised in Queens, NY, William John Rostron now splits his time between his home on Long Island and traveling the country in his Tiffin motorhome. He is busy completing a bucket list of travel adventures when not writing. In the past 20 years, he and his wife, Marilyn, have traveled 140,000 miles. These journeys have taken them to the 48 contiguous states, 133 national parks, all 30 major league baseball stadiums, 154 cities and towns, two Canadian provinces, and various unusual experiences and locations. Many of these locations have served as backgrounds for his books.

He is presently working on a fifth novel, *Dancing with the Lost,* which may be read independently or as the fifth book in *the Band in the Wind* series.

www.WilliamJohnRostron.com

ALSO BY WILLIAM JOHN ROSTRON

BOOKS

Band in the Wind

Sound of Redemption

Brotherhood of Forever

The Other Side of the Wind

A Flamingo Under the Carousel

~

Writer's Digest Award-Winning Stories in *T-Rex Stole My Computer*

"Call Me T-Rex"

"Cat's in the Cradle"

"Senseless"

~

Writer's Digest Award-Winning Stories in *A Flamingo Under the Carousel*

"Ava's Bubble"

"Time is Here and Gone"

~

Short Films from *T-Rex Stole My Computer*

"The Last Chord"

"Senseless"

~

Short Films from *A Flamingo Under the Carousel*

"Pretty Flamingo"

"In the Garden of Eden"

"Fool on the Hill"

"Ava's Bubble"

∽

View on http://www.WilliamJohnRostron.com

A Special Dedication:

Welcome to the world and our extended family

Josephine Rose Rowley - *(Grand Niece)*

&

Wolfgang Everett Bechtol - *(Great Grand Nephew)*

www.ingramcontent.com/pod-product-compliance
Lightning Source LLC
Chambersburg PA
CBHW051823040426
42447CB00006B/339